URBAN MYSTIC

URBAN MYSTIC

Recollections of Goswami Kriyananda

Ray Grasse

Inner Eye Publications | Chicago, Illinois 2019

Also by Ray Grasse:

The Waking Dream: Unlocking the Symbolic Language of Our Lives

Signs of the Times: Unlocking the Symbolic Language of World Events

Under a Sacred Sky: Essays on the Philosophy and Practice of Astrology

An Infinity of Gods: Conversations with an Unconventional Mystic, the Teachings of Shelly Trimmer

Copyright © 2019 Ray Grasse

First Edition 2019

All rights reserved. No part of this book may be used or reproduced in any manner (with the exception of quotations embodied in critical articles or reviews) without written permission from the author and publisher.

Cover photo copyright Ray Grasse
Cover design by Christine Ciancosi
Typeset by Amnet Systems

Inner Eye Publications | Chicago, Illinois

ISBN 13: 9781091971165

Your everyday life is *your spiritual life.*

— Goswami Kriyananda

TABLE OF CONTENTS

Acknowledgments — xi
Author's Preface — xiii

Part 1: The Man and the Mystic — 1
Part 2: Passages — 19
Part 3: Conversations. — 49

About the Author — 97

ACKNOWLEDGEMENTS

I'd like to extend a deep thanks to all those who offered feedback or assistance in the completion of this book, including Eileen Ruffer, Eric and Devi Klein, Marcia Sacks, Judith Wiker, Barbara Keller, Jim Chase, Laurence Hillman, William Hunt, Debby Sher, Sharon George, Gale Ahrens, Ed Maslovicz, Sue Neill, Sharon Steffensen, George and Lynda Gawor, Perry Fotopolous and David Blair. I also wish to express my gratitude to the Urania Trust for their support with my work.

AUTHOR'S PREFACE

Shortly after finishing my book on the yogi and mystic Shelly Trimmer, *An Infinity of Gods*, someone asked me why I didn't publish a book about Goswami Kriyananda first, since he was the teacher I studied with originally, and who introduced me to Shelly.*
I'd never given that much thought, but it took only a few seconds to realize the decision was due to something very practical, which centered around the fact that my interaction with the two teachers had been dramatically different, in very mundane ways.

My contact with Shelly consisted of a limited series of in-person meetings and long-distance communications, the latter mainly by cassette tape. As a result, when I went to write a book on him it was a relatively simple matter, since all I had to do was transcribe the tapes and organize the transcripts. In the case of Kriyananda, my studies were spread out over almost 15 years and involved numerous private conversations (most of them not recorded), attending hundreds of lectures, and reading various books he'd written. So precisely because the body of information I had to draw on was

---

* There are several teachers in the yogic tradition named "Kriyananda" (most notably, the late Swami Kriyananda of California, AKA J. Donald Walters, with whom the Chicago-born Kriyananda is sometimes confused). A simple way to distinguish the two teachers is through their titles: the Kriyananda I'm profiling in this book was known by the honorific *Goswami*, rather than *Swami*.

far more sprawling and diffuse, writing up an account of those interactions proved to be a considerably more complicated affair.

In the pages that follow you'll find the results of that compilation, which I've divided into three parts. The first is comparatively autobiographical and describes how I came to meet him, while describing some of the experiences I had with him through the years. Part two offers an assortment of key sayings and quotations of his that have been especially meaningful to me. Part three offers select passages from some of the recorded conversations I had with him during our time together. As a result this book isn't intended to be a definitive biography so much as a personal perspective on the man and his teachings. It's my hope that someday a biographer will set about writing a more detailed account of his life and legacy, but until then this book will hopefully open at least a window onto the contributions of someone whose influence loomed large in my own life. I hope it proves meaningful for you as well.

—Ray Grasse, 2019

PART I
THE MAN AND THE MYSTIC

In the months leading up to my 20th birthday, I wrestled mightily with the notion of linking up with a spiritual teacher. After the Beatles, Donovan and the Beach Boys traveled to India and did just that, it became somewhat fashionable in those days to seek out a guru. Indeed, more than a few writers at the time went so far as to assert that if you entertained any hope of finding "enlightenment," you'd better align yourself with a spiritual teacher—or you might as well just forget about it.

But the thought of putting myself at the feet of a guru troubled me, for any number of reasons. One of those involved a certain fear of commitment, since I thought that discipleship meant aligning yourself with a teacher for eternity. What if you picked the wrong teacher? But I also worried about the possibility of sacrificing my individuality, since I (mistakenly) feared that was part and parcel of the process. Besides, didn't the Buddha attain enlightenment on his own? Formal discipleship or not, I knew I wanted to acquire some of the knowledge offered by these teachers, should the chance ever arise.

As it turned out, that chance did arise. During sophomore year in college, a fellow student told me about an American-born swami in the area who was supposedly knowledgeable in the ways of mysticism and meditation. He called his center the Temple of Kriya Yoga, and it was located then on the fifth floor of an office building on State Street in downtown Chicago. Despite my nervousness about entering this new environment—I was fairly agoraphobic at the time, so social gatherings were a source of anxiety for me—I finally attended one of his lectures to see for myself what this man had to offer.

I was 19 years old at the time, and felt very out of place sitting there amongst those strangers, some of whose behaviors and appearances were very different from mine. I had no problem with the long-hair or the flowing dresses, but I was a bit wary of the bearded men with beads around their necks who brandished inscrutable smiles. Did that look imply peace of mind, or rather a cult-like mind-*less* ness? Kriyananda—or as the others referred to him, *Goswami* Kriyananda—certainly looked the part of a guru, with his long beard and flowing hair. He spoke that first night for a little over an hour, and his knowledge of mystical subjects was impressive. So impressive, in fact, that before I knew it I'd attended his classes and lectures for nearly 15 years in all.

Over the course of those years I became marginally involved with the Temple itself, volunteering my time to help design logos or advertisements, joining one or another committee to help plan out events, and on a handful of occasions teaching classes. Yet I was never compelled to take the final plunge and become a formal disciple, unlike most of the others. That proved to be a double-edged sword, for reasons that should become clearer as my story moves along.

It wasn't long before I learned his original name was Melvin Higgins. He was born in 1928, and lived most of his life up to then in the Chicagoland area. (As for why he never relocated elsewhere, he once remarked, "I believe one should bloom where one is planted.") He graduated from college, worked as in the business world for a while, and acquired a following of students that expanded in size as his center changed locations around the city. He first taught out of his home on Chicago's south side, in Hyde Park, after which he moved to several locations in the downtown Chicago area, finally relocating the Temple in 1979 to the Logan Square neighborhood on the city's north side.

He was notably unpretentious, and drove an old car at a time when some other better-known teachers were flaunting their conspicuous wealth in the form of multiple Rolls-Royces and phalanxes of fawning attendants. He also made himself surprisingly accessible to students after lectures, which also wasn't a common practice among teachers of his caliber. It was relatively easy walking into his office and approaching him with pressing concerns, and there was almost always a line of students outside his office looking for answers to their questions or for emotional support.

Despite that ease of access, it took me almost a full year to build up the nerve to go in and speak with him, one-on-one, since I was initially intimidated by his presence. When I finally did approach him, however, he couldn't have been friendlier. Over those next few years we wound up carrying our conversations outside the Temple, enjoying talks over lunch or dinner, while running errands in the city together or talking on the phone.

Indeed, the fact that I *wasn't* a disciple seemed to make it easier for him to be relatively open with me, since he wasn't as obliged to play the formal teacher/disciple role with me and maintain the disciplinary posture that often entails. He was always down-to-earth in our exchanges, never pious or ethereal, and it wasn't unusual for him to spruce up our conversations with a well-chosen expletive now and then. He was definitely a Chicago-born teacher, no doubt about it—and that was all for the better, far as I was concerned.

And every chance I had to speak with him over the years, I soaked up as much information as I could about subjects like karma, mythology, ancient history, astrology, meditation, comparative religion, or even politics. And he never held back, no matter how persistent or annoying I could be (which could be pretty persistent and annoying). I was especially impressed by how open he was about his own imperfections. It was obvious he didn't want to appear better than anyone else. Like his own guru, Shelly, he didn't wear his spirituality on his sleeve.

But I also suspect that low-keyed style may have affected his popularity and fame as a teacher in some ways. That's because some of the more well-known spiritual teachers making the rounds at the time projected a carefully cultivated air of "holiness" and solemn unapproachability that many interpreted as signs of spiritual merit—whether they actually possessed any or not. This wasn't Kriyananda's style at all. He could be self-effacing, often humorous, and very human. Yet underlying that humanness was a spiritual depth and core integrity that was obvious to me. On countless occasions, for example, I watched as he went out of his way to help others, sometimes at considerable expense or inconvenience to himself. At bottom, he struck me as a profoundly sensitive soul with a deep compassion for others.

I suspect some of that sensitivity may have come from experiencing a hard life while growing up. Before he was five, his father died and his mother remarried a man who ushered several more children into an already large household, with young Melvin now having to shoulder much of the responsibility of helping to raise those younger siblings. He openly admitted to being so shy when younger that he could hardly speak in social settings, something which undoubtedly pained him greatly. I had the sense his way of coping back then was escaping into books and learning as much as he could about spirituality, science, and history.

Over the years I interacted with him, he displayed a work ethic that confounded me in terms of its sheer energy. He gave formal lectures at least twice a week, on Sunday afternoons and Wednesday evenings, this being in addition to continuously offering courses on various subjects which extended anywhere from six weeks to twelve months, along with rigorous programs specifically designed for disciples and aspiring swamis. All of that was on top of an astrological practice that had him seeing clients five or six days a week, while he also churned out a series of books and pamphlets. I never quite figured out how he managed to do it all, and suspected he must have gotten by on just a few hours of sleep every night.

What kept him going? Though I knew he was passionate about teaching, I also knew the entire process wasn't always a stroll in the park. In particular, keeping the Temple afloat was an expensive endeavor and generated a mountain of bills—and he was the one mainly responsible for paying them. He once told the story about how exciting it was when he first opened the Temple, but then how challenging it became after a few years, not just financially but overseeing the parade of personalities that streamed through it. When he mentioned this to his own guru, the elder teacher responded, "Kriyananda, it's very easy to *create* something, whether that be a marriage, a business, or a temple. But it's much harder to *sustain* that creation." But sustain it he did, in the process affecting the lives of many thousands of men and women, both directly and indirectly.

The Teachings

He lectured on an wide range of esoteric and spiritual topics, but had a particular genius when it came to astrology. He was a virtual encyclopedia of information on both Eastern and Western astrological systems, and often discussed interpretive techniques I'd never heard of before, and to this day am still unsure where he learned them. Just as impressive was his hands-on talent for reading horoscopes. Much of the time Kriyananda seemed to have nearly X-Ray vision when it came to deciphering birth charts and what they revealed about their owners. I know of instances where he said things to individuals that were accurate in detailed ways that continue to baffle me, since I could find nothing in those horoscopes which prompted those insights.

Yet the central core of his teachings revolved principally around Kriya Yoga, a holistic tradition known for consciousness-raising techniques and a comparatively "householder" approach toward spiritual practice. With the notable exception of Paramahansa Yogananda, famed author of *Autobiography of a Yogi*, most of the teachers in this branch of the Kriya lineage were married and held regular jobs while teaching students. That was a definite plus far as I was concerned, since I certainly wasn't interested in celibacy. Kriyananda—or Melvin, as he was known early in life—first encountered the teachings of Kriya Yoga up close and personal through a mysterious teacher in Minnesota named Shelly Trimmer, who I'd eventually encounter myself (and who I wrote about in my book *An Infinity of Gods*).

With both his Sun and Moon in Taurus, there was a notable practicality to Kriyananda's teachings that was somewhat less pronounced in Shelly's sometimes more "cosmic" perspective. He had a talent for distilling complex spiritual doctrines into simple terms, such as this gem: "Everyone is trying to find God when they haven't even found their humanness yet." In that respect Kriyananda shared a close affinity with the here-and-now emphasis of Zen Buddhism (he once even remarked that Paul Reps' book *Zen Flesh, Zen Bones* was "one of the greatest books ever written").

That subtle difference between his spiritual perspective and Shelly's was apparent in a comment he once made about something the older guru said to him. On one occasion Shelly remarked how he never felt entirely comfortable in his physical body. "Other people are trying to get out of their physical body, but I have trouble staying in mine," Shelly said laughingly. In contrast with that perspective, Kriyananda took a more Zen-like approach when he said, "That's one of the few areas where I respectfully disagree with my guru. I believe that we should be comfortable *wherever* we find ourselves, whether that be in a 20-room mansion or a tiny shack."

There were a few other ways in which Kriyananda and Shelly differed in their approach toward teaching. For instance, Shelly had a pronounced trickster streak and was known to pull the wool over students' eyes—a teaching tactic Kriyananda found himself on the receiving end more than once. Directly as a result of those sometimes-frustrating lessons, he consciously chose to go in a different direction with students, once saying to me, "Ask me a question, and I'll shoot straight from the hip, I'll give you a direct answer."

But another key difference between them was in their approach concerned the matter of *legacy*. Shelly's modesty about his own contribution to the world was such that he felt no pressing desire to write books or preserve his ideas for posterity, other than teaching in that distinctly low-keyed, one-on-one fashion of his. Shelly genuinely seemed to believe that, in the greater scheme of things, his words ultimately meant very little. "If I don't do it or say it, someone else undoubtedly will," he once remarked. In contrast with that proverbial view from 30,000 feet, Kriyananda's had a more practical, boots-on-the-ground attitude. Early on, he set about working to preserve his ideas not only in books but through creating a library of audio tapes and videos that could be accessed online and that would survive long after he had passed.

Which of those two perspectives is the "right" one, Kriyananda's or Shelly's? To my mind, both are. They were simply different approaches, each with its own validity and value. Kriyananda and Shelly viewed the world through different lenses, set to very different magnifying powers, and I drew enormous value from both of them.

Kriyananda the Mystic
Of the varied insights I gathered from Kriyananda over the years, I especially valued those of a more personal nature, when he related experiences he had as an early student or later on as a teacher. Indeed, of all the teachings I've heard delivered by various

teachers over the years, it's intriguing to me how the ones that stand out most vividly in my memory are those of a more personal nature, even more than their philosophical ruminations. That was true with Kriyananda, too. As just one example, I recall a series of lectures Kriyananda delivered on Taoist philosophy sometime during the late 1970s, yet to this day the only thing I remember from that six-week course was a personal anecdote he shared in passing about a conversation he had with his own teacher, and which remains as vivid to me now as the day I heard it.

Most of these personal anecdotes were of a spiritual nature, describing some struggle or lesson he learned while growing up, or during some encounter with his guru. But a few of the more intriguing tales involved anecdotes of a psychic or paranormal nature. Why did those interest me? Because they suggested there was more going on with the man than meets the eye.

Curiously enough, Kriyananda strongly discouraged students from becoming overly concerned with psychic abilities or "magical powers." Indeed, it was one of the reasons he never recommended Yogananda's famed book *Autobiography of a Yogi* to new students, since he felt its emphasis on exotic powers and experiences misrepresented the spiritual path in certain respects. Yet he never denied those abilities existed, and on rare occasions spoke about his own paranormal experiences. While it's impossible for me to judge the ultimate validity of these accounts, I never sensed the slightest hint of ego or dishonesty in their telling—and as I'll explain shortly, I had reasons of my own to believe they were more than just fabrications.

Many of those stories were brief and simple, and casually mentioned in the course of longer lectures or conversations. One simple example was the time he spoke about driving along the city's outer drive that morning and seeing a dead dog lying alongside the road. He described perceiving the spirit of the dog wandering around the accident scene, looking dazed and confused as to what had happened to it. Feeling compassionate for the dog, he stopped his car along the shoulder of the busy road to tend to it, blessing it and sending it on its way.

Or the time he was drafted into the army during the Korean War where he served as a medic and found himself situated near the battlefront. While huddling in the trench during one conflict, he described seeing a fellow soldier rise up and march towards enemy lines, only to be shot and instantly killed. But while the soldier's body dropped to the ground, Kriyananda said he saw the man's astral double keep marching forward, as though he hadn't realized he'd been fatally shot.

Once he spoke of attending a Catholic church service that was being conducted by a priest who he'd been friends with. Normally, he explained, he would sit in the back of a church and see the energies of the parishioners during the service; whenever the priest would lift the chalice upwards at that point of communion, he'd usually see the spinal currents of everyone rise upwards as well, as if in sympathetic resonance with the ritual up on the altar.

But on this particular Sunday morning, the priest lifted the chalice upwards—and nothing happened in the spines of the parishioners; no subtle energies were stirred. Curious as to the difference this time, he spoke to his priest friend after the service and inquired whether there was anything different about the ceremony this particular Sunday. It turned out the church had run out of wine, so the priest substituted grape juice instead that day. Kriyananda used this story to illustrate the importance of symbolic "purity" in rituals and the need to use the appropriate ingredients to embody one's intentions.

Then there was this. One afternoon in 1978 Kriyananda emerged from his office to deliver his usual Sunday afternoon talk, but he was looking noticeably disturbed about something. Sitting down before the podium, he shook his head back and forth gently a few times and muttered softly, "They're doing some *crazy things* down there..."—with no further explanation. He continued on with his talk, leaving myself and the others in attendance perplexed about that opening comment. What did he mean by "down there"? Or by "crazy things"? I continued wondering about it, so after his talk I headed downstairs to the lower floors of the hotel lobby to see if he might have been referring to something taking place down there, or even outside the building. But I found nothing unusual at all.

Later that evening, I turned on the TV to hear reporters talk about news trickling in from South America about a mass suicide down in Guyana. Over the next few days, reports revealed that over 900 residents of Jonestown had taken their lives under the direction of cult leader Jim Jones—and it had all started unfolding around the time of Kriyananda's talk. Was he psychically sensing the mass tragedy happening far away? There's no way to know for sure, but that was the only time I ever heard him make a public comment like that.

There were even some possible instances of prophecy. One of them involved a young woman named Karen Phillips, a disciple of his and a good friend of mine from the suburban town I was living in, Oak Park. While lecturing privately to his disciples one day (as related to me later that week by his disciple, Bill Hunt), Kriyananda made this sobering remark: "In six weeks one of you will no longer be with us." Was he implying someone was going to move out of state? Or something more serious? Most of those in attendance that afternoon had no idea what to make of the statement, and probably just forgot about it after a few days. But I was intrigued enough on hearing about it that I carefully kept an eye on the calendar to see if any of his disciples might be departing the Temple in six weeks.

Exactly six weeks later I walked into the Temple to attend a class when a phone call came in to the front desk. The receptionist picked it up, and on the other end of the line was someone saying that Karen Phillips had been brutally murdered the night before. As the receptionist broke the news to Kriyananda, he looked concerned but not surprised. Eventually, the case received worldwide media coverage, because of one singularly odd element: the culprit was identified as a young Bible student living several doors down from Karen, who went to the police shortly afterwards to describe a dream in which he witnessed precise details of the murder. Because of how closely the dream matched the actual crime, he was arrested and eventually convicted of the murder, spending several years in jail before his conviction was finally overturned on appeal.

It was the only time I heard Kriyananda ever make a prediction that dramatic, and I naturally wondered how he arrived at it. Years later, though, Kriyananda may have provided a clue when a local magazine interviewed him and asked how anyone could verify whether an astral projection experience was valid or just a fantasy. He answered by describing his own early experiences with astral projection, and what he learned from them:

I (eventually) encountered disembodied souls who told me about their children and what was going to happen to them. Years later, these events manifested exactly the way the parents said they would. This evidence absolutely confirmed the afterlife's existence and its link to human earth life and earth life to the afterlife. It was those experiences that removed any remaining doubt that humans were able to see into the afterlife.

Interesting stories all, no doubt. But how could I be sure they weren't anything more than just coincidence, or fabrications? The answer is, I can't—not positively anyway. But in some instances the unusual phenomena I witnessed *did* involve me directly, in which case they took on an entirely different weight for me. Here are a couple of examples of those.

Consider the time I had a conversation with Goswami Kriyananda and posed a series of questions to him on a variety of subjects, while I recorded his comments on the battery-powered tape recorder I'd placed on his desk, where it remained near to me and never within his reach. One of those questions I asked him concerned the existence of God, and he may well have given me a fascinating answer; but unfortunately I was so busy checking the next question on my sheet that I barely noticed what he was saying. When I finally looked up from my paper, there was a look on his face of mild exasperation, as though he could tell I wasn't really paying attention and was too caught up figuring out my next query. On top of that, he shook his head slightly and muttered something to the effect that, "I really shouldn't have said quite so much..." I wasn't too worried, though, since I'd been recording the conversation and knew I could always listen to his answers once I'd returned home—right?

But before I left the building that day, Kriyananda did something odd. He came up to me and said, "Wait a second, Ray, can I see that tape?" Sure, I said, as I pulled out the cassette tape and handed it over. Grasping it with one hand, he proceeded to quickly rub the cassette tape two or three times with his index and middle fingers, then handed it back to me with an almost mischievous look on his face. As he turned and walked away from me, I could only wonder what *that* was all about.

That night at home, I excitedly sat down to listen to the tape, and was especially interested to hear that one section of the conversation where I asked him about God. But lo and behold, when I got to that part of the tape, it was blank. Exactly as I expected to hear him answer my question, there was no sound on the tape at all, only silence. Then, right at the point where I launched into my *next* question, the sound on the tape mysteriously started up again. That silent spot was the only blank patch on the entire recording.

I was baffled, and started to mentally retrace my steps from earlier in the day to see if there was any conceivable way he could have done something to the tape or the recorder to make that glitch occur. But the recorder was in my possession the entire time, and was running on batteries rather than via any power cord. He never once touched it. Still skeptical about what happened, the next time I walked into the Temple and saw him, I asked right off, "Okay....now, how did you *do* that?" From the look on his face, it was obvious he knew exactly what I was referring to, but he just laughed and walked away.

Then there was this. Throughout much of that period I struggled with meditation, often feeling as though I was simply spinning my wheels in the backwaters of conventional mind. I saw others sitting quietly and motionless during their meditations, but I usually felt frustrated by my own restlessness and inability to go very deep in my meditations. But for one short but unusually fruitful stretch of time, I seemed to "strike gold" with one Kriya technique known as the *Hong Sau* mantra. This is a silent, strictly internal mantra that is coupled with one's breathing pattern. For that relatively brief span of time, things came together for me in a powerful way, to where I felt as though I finally "got" what the technique was about—or at least one aspect of what it was about (since a given technique doesn't necessarily have a single intended outcome). Each time I engaged this technique I experienced a heightening of awareness along with a welling up of blissful energy that was dramatic, and deeply pleasurable.

During one of Kriyananda's talks, I was sitting in the back of the dimly lit room and began practicing the Hong Sau technique. My eyes were closed, and I was completely silent, with nothing externally to indicate what I was doing internally. Then, shortly after I began feeling that surge of blissful energy in me, I heard Kriyananda stop lecturing in mid-sentence and go completely silent for about 15 seconds. That wasn't at all normal for him during a talk, so I opened my eyes to see what was going on—only to see him peering through the darkness directly at me, as everyone else in the room now turned to see what he was looking at. Embarrassed by the sudden attention, with all eyes now directed at me, I stopped the technique, and Kriyananda resumed his lecture as if nothing had happened.

Exactly one week later, a friend of mine (who didn't know I was using that technique) happened to walk into Kriyananda's office to ask if he would teach him the Hong-Sau mantra. Kriyananda replied, "Why don't you ask Ray to teach it to you? He seems to be having some pretty good luck with it." When my friend told me of that exchange, I was floored, not only because it indicated Kriyananda knew I was having a powerful meditation that afternoon, but even pinpointed the exact technique I was using. *That* was impressive, I thought.

Instances like those led me to accept the possibility he did in fact possess unusual psychic abilities. During one conversation with him about my own inability to intuit people's intentions, I light-heartedly said, "We can't all be as psychic as you, Kriyananda!" To which he claimed he wasn't born that way, and that while young was about as "un-psychic as anyone could be." Being an earthy double-Taurus, he added, he originally believed if one couldn't touch, taste, or measure something, it just wasn't real. The implication there seemed to be that it was a result of extensive meditations over the years that his intuitive powers developed as far as they had.

Yet I also suspect those unusual potentials may well have been latent from birth, just waiting to be triggered. I say that for this reason. I took a course in palmistry from him at one point in the 1970s, and in one class he used his hand to make a point about the length and shape of the lines in the palm, and what these meant from a symbolic standpoint. It was then that I happened to notice something very unusual about the little finger on his right hand—the finger associated by astrologers and palmists with the mind, as well as the planet Mercury. Instead of the usual three joints, his little finger had *four*. That was surprising, so I asked him whether that indicated unusual mental capacities. He laughed and humbly played it down, saying, "Yes, but remember, I'm left-handed, so the usual view that the left hand shows inborn potentials and the right hand shows what you've done with them is reversed in my case!" I frankly didn't quite buy his humble revision of traditional palmistry theory, but revision or not, it was an anomalous anatomical feature I'd never seen on anyone's hand before, nor for that matter since.

The Final Years
Unfortunately, despite a few peak moments here and there, my own attempts at meditation were unfolding at a snail's pace, and more often than not I struggled with simply sitting still. The longer I studied at the Temple, the more I realized how much work I still needed to do in that respect—which is when I began entertaining the possibility of taking part in a longer-term meditation retreat somewhere away from the Temple. Thus it was in late 1986 that I went off to live for several months at Zen Mountain Monastery in upstate New York, where I managed to learn a few more helpful things about meditation.

But I kept in touch with Kriyananda over the coming years, calling him on occasion or traveling into the city to meet him in his office. For me, one of the main values of having access to a spiritual teacher is the chance to get honest feedback about one's own spiritual or psychological progress—however painful that can be at times. Had he been my actual guru, I suspect he would have taken an even stricter stance with me and offered more explicit suggestions about how to enhance my practice; and had that happened, I have no doubt I would have grown much faster and farther than I did, spiritually. But simply being able to get any of his feedback on my life and mind from time to time was immensely valuable. So just as I had always done during the years I attended talks at the Temple, I would ask, "Where do you think I most need to work on myself now?" Generally, he would calmly but compassionately respond with comments like, "You lack self-discipline" (which was true); or "You're too much in your head, Ray" (also true), or "You need to meditate more" (very true, too)—and other pointed observations.

But on some occasions, he'd extend a touching compliment out of the blue, and those were meaningful in a different way. For instance, I came to know a student of his named Rebecca Romanoff, with whom I spent much time over the years as friends. We would get together for lunch or dinner sometimes, sit along the lakefront, or go to see a movie. Eventually, many years later, some time after his first wife died from cancer, Kriyananda and Rebeccca got married, and they lived together until her death in 2013.

But in 1983, a couple of years prior to their marriage, she invited Kriyananda and myself over to her apartment for dinner, where we spent the evening talking about a wide variety of subjects. At one point, I began reminiscing with Rebecca about some of the activities we enjoyed doing back in the old days, at which point she interjected, very self-critically, "Oh, you must have thought I was such a basket case back then."

I was genuinely surprised to hear how hard she was on herself—especially considering I always regarded *her* as the one who had it together, and that *I* had been the neurotic one, not her. So I quickly responded, "Oh, Becky! I've never judged you like that!" At which point Kriyananda chimed in unexpectedly, "You know, that's something you and Shelly have in common; you're the two individuals I know who aren't at all judgmental towards others." To be compared like that with his teacher—even in such a modest way—was deeply moving, especially coming at a time when I was dealing with a string of personal disappointments in my life.

In the summer of 2013 I received the sad news that Rebecca had passed away. It was around that time I decided to preserve what I could of the teachings I'd gathered from both Kriyananda and Shelly, as I began sorting through the records of my years studying with them. In Kriyananda's case, that involved searching through several dozen notebooks I'd compiled from which I selected key passages and quotes which I felt distilled his teachings in more digestible form. As it so happened, virtually the same day I finished that selection and posted those quotes online, April 21, 2015, I received word that Kriyananda himself passed away, having lived out his last days in France. I'd sent him a message just two weeks earlier to get his approval on what I had compiled, just to make sure I wasn't misrepresenting his thoughts in any way. When I didn't hear back from him, I was perplexed, since he normally responded fairly quickly. When I received word of his passing, though, I realized he probably wasn't in any condition to communicate with me at that point.

What follows is the result of that compilation.

PART II
PASSAGES

In the process of going back over my handwritten notes taken down during my years of attending Kriyananda's talks, I was struck by the number of pithy statements he made during those discourses —gem-like bits of wisdom often delivered in an offhand, spontaneous way. Indeed, I even suspect this could wind up being one of his greatest legacies: that ability to distill profound teachings into a few simple words, which invite extended contemplation.

I've assembled some of my favorites from amongst those sayings, along with a few memorable ones drawn from published sources such as magazine interviews or books. Because many of my own were jotted down hurriedly at the time or reconstructed from memory afterwards, the exact wording may be slightly off at times, but never to the point of distorting the spirit of the original comments. While these don't substitute for his more extended lectures, classes, or books, of course, they do serve as useful points of entry into those broader teachings, and on that level have a value all their own.

There can be no such thing as 'failure' if you do what you do because you enjoy it.

Everyone's striving for God, when they haven't even found their humanness yet.

Life itself is the Self.

It's easy to become illuminated, it's hard to become happy.

Every thought going through our mind either saps or strengthens us.

You are a *part of* life, not *apart from* life.

Recognize that everything you see is part of you.

No effort is ever lost. Whatever effort you apply towards a dream, whether that be spiritual or worldly in nature, all adds up karmically.

Every moment of your life is a rebirth. Act and think accordingly.

Whatever you want to get more of *from* life, give more of that *to* the world.

If you're going to do something, do it—and enjoy it. I once visited a friend in the hospital who was dying of lung cancer who had smoked cigars his entire life. I asked him if he had any regrets about that habit. He said, "No, I really don't. I enjoyed every minute of smoking those cigars." Now, *that's* a spiritual attitude.

Getting your insights or enlightenment should be through a methodology, not by accident. Drugs can bring insights, but not a permanent understanding. It's like stumbling onto the solution to a Rubik's cube as opposed to having a repeatable methodology for solving it.

You can take a positive feeling towards one thing and direct it towards something you don't like, to help neutralize it.

We are encased in a bodily cocoon of many lifetimes' worth of karmas.

There really is no 'outer' or 'inner' world. There is only one world.

Think of the one thing you could erase from your life if you could, in terms of your past mistakes. You can then concoct an act or a sacrifice to compensate for it. But the act or sacrifice has to be proportional to the problem.

Meditation is not about becoming more energized or powerful. Meditation is a state of power*less*ness, of pure balance.

When you get lost underwater, don't struggle too much, because you may wind up swimming downwards. Relax and float up to the surface. Know that the laws of nature are on your side.

It's helpful, vibrationally, to keep plants in the rooms where you live and sleep.

Try to think of your life in terms of eons, in terms of many lifetimes. That's a good protective mechanism, because it puts all of your desires and actions into a larger context.

Karma is not necessarily spread out evenly among different lifetimes. A person can choose to "bundle up" a sizable amount of difficult karma into one incarnation, but in the next lifetime compensate by taking it relatively easy, with what might be called an "rest and relaxation" lifetime, with a horoscope that has lots of trines. Your karmic load can vary tremendously from lifetime to lifetime.

The higher up you go in levels of reality, the more time dissolves, and the harder it is to see causal relationships.

The greater the sage, the simpler they will tend to be.

Be not the bearer of another's difficult karma.

In preparing for sleep, try to picture all of the body's energies drawing in from your limbs, into the center of the spine, and going up the spine.

When falling asleep, arouse an intense desire to attract higher forces. And vow to keep continuity of consciousness.

When you are asleep, your astral body floats about two and a half to three feet above your physical body. A horizontal spine symbolizes relatively little self-conscious awareness, like an animal's normal spinal position. The symbol of the vertical spine is one of greater self-conscious awareness. We are trying to awaken the astral body's consciousness, to get it to stand upright and—when necessary—walk away from the physical body and, in turn, physical experiences, thereby bringing us into subtler worlds and experiences.

Realize that when you're angry it's actually just one of your chakras that is angry.

Each chakra has a mind of its own.

Your interpretation of an experience is more powerful than the experience itself.

Even if you can't neutralize all of the karmas indicated by your horoscope, there's always the neutralizing force of *attitude*. The largest portion of karma is actually our response to it. Why is it one person loses a leg and can still be happy, while another breaks their fingernail and feels like it's the end of the world?

Don't let another's negativity overpower your compassion for them.

(In response to the question, "How do mystics deal with boredom?") A mystic is never bored.

The delay factor inherent in the material or "Saturn" plane may be frustrating but it's actually a blessing. Think back over your life and imagine if all of your desires had instantaneously become reality.

We will not die, we cannot die. We are immortal. Every dream, goal and desire that people have will be fulfilled. It may take another 100,000 lifetimes, or it may manifest in this lifetime. But if we give up and say, "Well, I'm going to die in another 10 years, 20 years, or 30 years, what's the use of it all," then people won't row their boat, they won't progress at all. People just do not understand that they are immortal, they think they are their body. And we have to learn patience. All things that are worthwhile take time.

Part of one's diet is the eating of air.

If you want to take credit for all your good karmas, then you have to be willing to take credit for all your problematic karmas, too.

The single most important thing to realize about astral travel is, you don't actually *go* anywhere. That's because you already *are* everywhere. It's really just a matter of shifting your attention from one part of yourself to another.

How does one develop will power? By using it.

Thought forms are, for the most part, asymmetrical, impure, rough, not a singular energy. By contrast, mantras are relatively pure, relatively symmetrical, which gives them more power.

Mantras help to wash off successive layers of thought.

You can look down from the vantage point of the Ajna chakra (the "third eye") and see everybody else's material and mental realms. From that vantage point you see an infinite number of sidereal universes, and that surrounding each spark of God is built a universe.

God enters and exits with every breath.

You were here long before the solar system.

It's important to know your desires and compulsions from your spiritual intentions. How can you tell which of your decisions are consciously willed, and which are just desire-motivated? If it comes easy, it's probably desire.

Dedication to one thing is the primary discipline on the path.

We're usually lying to ourselves about our real motives for doing things. We say 'I want to get married *because...*' or 'I want to become famous *because...*,' but we don't really know why. Look deeper.

People may be angry at their mother, father, spouse, boss, or even the president of the United States, but what they are really fighting are the thoughts in their own head. This doesn't mean you no longer take action in the world, simply that you know what your true motivations are.

Most of us are simply coasting on past karmas. Many of us need to put our foot on the accelerator and energize our minds!

Overcome your hang-ups about touching dead flesh. Otherwise, when you die, your subconscious will recoil at the process.

How you see the world depends to a great degree on what's in your stomach. When you pull away from food, things don't have the same power. Fast for a few days then try turning on a TV, and you'll see how differently it affects you.

When you feel something negative coming around you, imagine being surrounded by a golden aura.

Thoughts and emotions aren't bad. *Hanging onto* them is what gets us into trouble.

You have a conscious mind and five subconscious minds.

The symbols in your dreams, however inanimate they might seem, can literally talk. Ask them questions. Their answers may be untrue, in a purely factual sense, but they'll tell you a great deal about your own consciousness. In one's waking life as well, you can talk to anything in the universe, and it will talk back to you—if you can hear.

A disorganized life is spiritually detrimental.

Mystics are never nationalists.

One can incarnate into the past by going into a sidereal universe similar to this one, where the events are further back in sequence.

Eliminate your negative thoughts towards one thing and you eliminate them towards a whole complex of things in your subconscious, because all symbols are interconnected.

(Regarding astral travel) If you're not glowing, you're still in the lower realms.

You can learn from suffering, but the mystic prefers to learn through wisdom. Does an alcoholic really have to suffer from a diseased liver to learn that drinking might be bad for them? Let wisdom and knowledge be your teacher, not pain.

Spiritual growth comes from self-discipline.

One way or another, your karma has to manifest. But you can choose to manifest it *symbolically*.

People ask, if reincarnation is real then why don't we remember our past lives? We do, actually, but more in terms of our emotional patterns.

The astral plane is practically all symbolic.

When you truly understand the wisdom of another, it becomes your own.

The Kriyic (spiritual) forces are more pronounced and accessible at the moment of sunrise and sunset, as well as during the Spring and Autumnal equinoxes. That's because these are points of balance, when the male and female forces of Ida and Pingala are relatively evened out.

Think of the Sun and Moon in the horoscope as objective and subjective amplifiers. Planetary aspects to the Moon will be felt more emotionally, but aspects to the Sun will manifest as actual conditions out there in the 'real' world.

A very important technique is to watch your thoughts, non-judgmentally. Close your eyes and with detachment, watch all the thoughts that come through your mind. Do this for a few minutes each day. This is extremely helpful towards helping you become detached from your thoughts. You can use the "Neti, Neti" technique where each time you perceive a thought, you say "I am not this thought, I am not that thought." Eventually, you may get to the point where you realize, "I am not *any* thought."

If you can slow yourself down three times a day, even if it's only for a second or two, that will still be extremely valuable. Keep your body completely still for those few moments.

There is no such thing as "group karma," really, just individuals who come together who have similar karma.

Find joy in your everyday living. *Everything* should bring you joy.

When you see beauty in the world, inhale, suck it in and raise it up through your spine to the 1000-petaled lotus, to the top of your head.

Kriya is a direct relationship of balancing what is inside you with that that is outside you. But anything can be a 'kriya.' *Kriya is the understanding of the relation of you to that which is before you.*

Change your mind and you change your destiny.

The challenge is to break free from our limiting thoughts. It's as though we live in a castle of a 108 rooms, and we spend our whole life in a basement compartment, thinking "This is life"—failing to realize or even conceive that there are 107 other rooms. Awaken! Open the door, move out, move up, visit the palace of your consciousness; and at some moment, you will open the front door to that palace, only to step out into the beauty that is life, putting to shame, truly, the glorious beauty of the palace in which you live.

The trident held by the sadhus (yogi ascetics) of India symbolizes that they are the masters of the three realms—the physical, astral, and the spiritual.

If you ever have the feeling that the area where you're living is being affected by someone's negative vibrations, or even by a negative thought form created by someone in the past, there is a simple technique you can do to help negate it. Turn on your tap water and imagine any negativity in the environment rushing down with that water. Running water can help dispel negative vibrations very rapidly, since the water absorbs those vibrations. Within a matter of seconds, you will feel the room clearing. Running water is a blessing. And rather than having it run down the drain with no sound, try to get the sound of water splashing—the water sound is important. You may even want to put a cup in the sink so that the water splashes, since that will intensify the purification process. (Notice how in the oriental system of *feng shui,* living near a source of running water—such as a river, fountain, or waterfall—is also considered auspicious, whereas stagnant water is to be avoided. - RG)

To share knowledge is the highest form of love.

When you see someone in pain and offer a blessing or a prayer for that person, you are drawn into that soul's world. Why do you feel their pain? In large part, it is because you are reacting to something inside of *you*. To truly help that person, you must remove the pain inside you—then and only then can they receive the full blessing. Within our isolated universes, it is the pain—or the joy or love or wisdom—that links us together. If that pain were not somehow within me, I would not be aware of it within you, nor would I react to it. Therefore, I send my meditation out to you, but first I have to heal my memory track inside of me. Then the energy can be released from my isolated universe and join with, and enter into, the isolated world of your universe.

We're comparatively aware of how our bodies consume and excrete substances, like food or liquids. And if we are sensitive, we may also be aware of the subtle vibrations of those substances. The secret is to realize that over and above that dense, in-food, out-food system of our body there is the larger one, especially the pore system, which absorbs the auras, vibrations, and thought forms in the environment we life in. So daily, before sleep in particular, and on awakening, send forth a positive thought form into the room you're in, and allow that thought form to expand out into the whole house or apartment, into the whole block, the whole city and into the whole world—but definitely into the area where you spend your time. And for most of us there are two areas in particular: one is the home environment, the other is the work environment. So daily send forth a positive thought form of light to dissolve the shadows and the darkness, send forth warmth to remove the damp and the mustiness, and send forth truth to defeat ignorance and forgetfulness.

In Samadhi, there is a oneness between you and the object on which you are meditating. If any superficial or secondary thought enters into your mind, in any language or symbol, it will immediately pull you out of your state of Samadhi and thus into a lower state of consciousness, into a more compounded state of consciousness.

When you have reached the state known as *Ananda Samadhi*, you are on the outer fringes of God-Realization. That is the Samadhi on joy, which is the tenth stage. In these higher states of *Ananda Samadhi*, things take on the fragrance of love, of ananda, and all things emanate that bliss. From then on, you will find yourself "smelling" the fragrance of the sky, the trees, the sun, and so on.

Some people feel that if you have the anandic Bliss, however, nothing else matters. And it is very easy to get lost in that Bliss and think, "Oh, how nice!" But you must break through even that Bliss sheath to find the Ultimate Reality. As my guru Shelly would say, if you are really trying to reach a state of illumination, you must penetrate the final barrier of God's "defense," so to speak—which is the barrier of love and of Bliss. Then you are really home, and this is where real wisdom comes.

You can go up to the higher astral and be deeply moved and inspired by your experience there, so that when you come back down you radiate this beauty out into your everyday life. But this change may not last if it hasn't really touched the deepest level of your being. But true samadhi does, true illumination does touch that deepest level, and that will last with you from lifetime to lifetime.

Mindfulness can be divided into two parts: mindfulness that brings *tranquility*, and mindfulness that brings *insight*. Usually these are the steps. But for some people they simply come to the point of tranquility and say, "Oh, this is nice!"—and they go no further. It's like being lost in the bliss of ananda. But then one realizes, *there are things to be done*. Of course, to sup upon the bliss is needed, to feel joy is needed, because these are the forces that heal the everyday mind so that we can then be released from it and move on to the higher mind. Yet there is the next step of reaching out to the mindfulness that brings *insight*, that brings insightful meditation, that brings insightful living. Which then leads us out of the mind states and into consciousness, and ultimately into cosmic consciousness.

Saturn is the great teacher. Whenever it crosses over any point or planet in your horoscope, you can see whether you've gotten it together and balanced out the energies in that area. If it triggers and disaster strikes, or you become overly emotional and upset, you know you've got more work to do. But if the result is more harmonious, it suggests you've likely done well in balancing out the energies in that part of your life.

Your everyday life *is* your spiritual life.

Every person who comes into your life, whether pleasant or unpleasant, is there to teach you, and offers you a process by which to neutralize karma that needs to be neutralized, to see what's wrong with your attitude, your thinking, your actions. And there are two ways that can happen: the long slow, painful way of living out again and again the negativity and emotionality of the past; or the way in which we finally say, "Let me awaken to and understand what is happening *in me*, and why this keeps happening—and to then adjust it." That is the fast path, the royal path, the path of yoga and the true mystic.

We must pull away from trying to change people, to "improve" people. What is the real motivation there? It's like the religious fundamentalist who, the more he really doubts at a deep level his own beliefs, the more fanatical he becomes in trying to convert the world to them, thinking that perhaps if he can convert enough people then those beliefs must be true and maybe he can accept them himself. As Shelly said to me, many of the problems in the world are caused by people trying to be "helpful." Mysticism is the realization that we need to take that time and energy we're directing at all those people and direct it back to our minds, to balance and spiritually heal our own consciousness and body. Why? At one level, it boils down to wanting to be happy, while for some it's about wanting to understand. At a deep mystical level, it stems from the realization that we really want to have control of our life—and that it's not about controlling other people or even the forces of nature, but rather about controlling the thoughts we think, to be aware of our thoughts. So with insight rather than judgment you learn to neutralize those negative patterns and instead choose to play on your "mental phonograph" a new song, a positive song, so that the outcome of your practice becomes that of contentment, fulfillment, and happiness.

As the old Hermetic teachings says, *All things are thrice compounded.* For example, take a pencil. What symbolic principle rules it? As a symbol of communication, it's obviously related to Mercury. As a sharp, pointed object, it also has the quality of Mars. But suppose the pencil has been used primarily to write love letters, which brings in the quality of Venus. We live in a compounded reality, and it takes great occult discernment to perceive the different meanings in any object, experience, or phenomenon.

This earth plane is not a plane of perfection, but it *is* a realm of completion.

The astral world is composed of many different sub-levels, but there are two main divisions which we call the "lower" astral and the "higher" astral. The dream world is part of the lower astral, to which most people have easy access. The difference between the lower and higher astral realms is that the lower levels have more emotionality and are more subjective in content. The higher the astral realm is, the less emotionality and thus more objective, noetic data it reveals. By analogy, the astral world is much like the ocean on a stormy day: the surface of the ocean is very turbulent, but the deeper you go, the less turbulence you find. Close to the bottom of the ocean there is little or no motion, little or no turbulence. Likewise the deeper (higher) into the astral you go, the calmer and less turbulence there is.

At times the dream world can seem senseless, but that's because we don't understand language it "speaks." When I was in Japan and China, I heard Westerners sometimes say that the language there made no sense and had no logic. But that was because of their inability to understand those languages. It is exactly the same when dealing with dreams and the symbols therein. They seem senseless only because we don't understand the language of dreams, we don't "speak" the language of symbolism. People haven't taken the time to learn and explore the language of dreams, which is actually the warp and weft that constitutes the fabric of our own inner consciousness.

We're actually dreaming 24 hours a day. What we normally call "dreaming" is simply what we've been able to recall from the sleep state. But dreaming is actually an ongoing, continual process.

The eagle of wisdom soars high above the dove of love. The mind should rule the heart, the heart should not rule the mind. As my guru said to me years ago, it is good that I should want to help others, but I must do so wisely, not foolishly or carelessly.

What you have become in life is determined by the major thoughts you have held in your mind, and what you'll become in the future will be determined by the major thoughts you hold in your mind now. But because we are all linked to one another by a sort of "morphogenetic" force field, it is important to recognize that our consciousness is also heavily conditioned and restricted by the families and groups that we align ourselves with.

There is a chakra in the back of your head which yogis call the Chandra chakra, that is a counterpart to the "third eye" in the forehead, or Ajna chakra. Yogananda referred to this chakra in the back of the head as the *Mouth of God*, because it's the portal through which we draw in the vital energy of the universe. When you breathe in, you inhale that vital energy or "prana" from the rest of the universe, and that current of energy moves down to the root chakra at the base of the spine, then back up again to the Sun chakra (or "third eye") on the exhale.

The two chakras at the head level, Ajna and Chandra, are really two poles of the same essential consciousness, like masculine and feminine, and are symbolized by the Sun and the Moon. In mythology, these represent the proverbial "land of milk and honey" that we are seeking in our spiritual quest. When those two poles are balanced out, when the observer becomes the observed and the lover becomes the beloved, this culminates in the "Royal Marriage," the joining of the Sun and the Moon, in which we realize our true nature.

When you're relaxed or meditating, the chakra in the back of your head opens up, which makes you much more sensitive to energies in the world. Drugs can open that chakra up, too, but in a way that is often extreme or even explosive, and that can lead to being spaced-out or overly sensitive to the vibrations around you. If that should occur, a simple yogic technique to help close that chakra is to press your tongue up against the inside of your upper teeth. On the other hand, to open that chakra you should curl your tongue back up into the mouth as far as possible (which is a practice also suggested in combination with many Kriya meditation techniques).

Think back over your whole life and ask: What one thing has most harassed you? What issue, concern or memory would improve your life most dramatically if you could remove it entirely from your consciousness? In my life I've very clearly had one terrible regret—I've had many regrets, actually (laughs), but one unbelievably awful regret—and when I first tried to neutralize it, the conditioning of my childhood immediately said to me, "No, no, that person's dead, there's nothing you can do about it." But the answer, thanks to the mystical teachings, was, "Yes, that person may be dead physically, but they're still alive in you as a thought form in one of your chakras. Find that chakra, Kriyananda, and ask forgiveness; find that chakra and atone; find that chakra and move upward with detachment, wisely, to your liberation and your freedom."

Your left nostril is related to the left-hand current of Ida, which is the subtle channel associated with emotions and the astral, while your right nostril is associated with the right-hand current of Pingala, the subtle channel associated with logic and the waking world. Certain yogic breathing techniques serve to manipulate the spinal currents by working with the right and left nostrils in various ways. For example, the practice of "alternate breathing" helps to bring those opposing currents into greater balance by regulating and balancing one's breathing through the two nostrils.

Similarly, when you bring the palms of your hands together, as in prayer or when saying "namaste" to another, you symbolically help balance the currents on the right and left sides of your nature and serve to bring those energies more into the central channel of your being.

Towards the end of his life, Kriyananda devoted considerable attention to the subject of death and dying, and how to best prepare for that final transition. His teachings on this were extensive and complex (a considerable body of which are still available on audio from the Temple of Kriya Yoga), but a few basic points and comments from those classes and conversations stand out in my memory, which I'll paraphrase here.

Probably the simplest method that the average person can employ to prepare for dying is to develop the habit of falling asleep slowly. Most individuals tend to quickly "black out" into unawareness once their head hits the pillow. But if one can learn to fall asleep slowly, one increases the chances of entering into the dream state—and the astral—more consciously. In turn, this increases your chances of remaining awake through the dying process as well, rather than simply blacking out into expanded unawareness.

Along related lines, one of the advantages of developing a meditation practice is to gradually increase your "samadhi"—that is, your ability to sustain heightened balanced awareness. This becomes especially valuable in the death and dying process because, similar to what happens when we fall asleep, it's easy to black out on entering higher and more expanded states of consciousness, where many are "blinded by the light," as it were. Meditation is a way of becoming more adjusted to, and familiar with, those expanded states of awareness. As Kriyananda expressed it, "By becoming more aware of our nature through meditation, not just physically but on subtler levels, we learn to sustain our mindfulness, improve that mindfulness, and direct energy towards the awakening of the astral body, until we can function within it, and function within those subtler states and levels of being."

Kriyananda recommended "sleep-fasting" at least once a month, preferably on the New or Full Moon. Here as well, it's a matter of learning to strengthen one's consciousness in the face of the countervailing forces of sleep. If one can remain awake in more ordinary contexts like this, it increases one's chances of remaining awake during that critical transition of bodily death, when the physical vehicle starts failing and one transitions into the light.

Like many other spiritual teachers, Kriyananda also emphasized the importance of not leaving this world with important business unfinished, whether that be anger towards others, unresolved regrets about career or family, or any deep emotional wounds. Towards that end, it's not only important to take stock of lingering issues from one's life but to spend some time each and every night to review the previous day and smooth out any unbalanced emotions, so as not to carry those energies into the astral state and in turn one's subconscious. This review process Kriyananda referred to as **tarka**. *Simply forgetting an issue doesn't mean it has been resolved, Kriyananda emphasized, and it's incumbent on us to clear up emotional problems as soon as possible before they set down roots.*

In contrast with some other spiritual teachers, Kriyananda suggested there was considerable value in learning to astral project, for reasons directly related to death and dying. Why? Because by learning to leave one's body consciously prior to death, one realizes one really isn't just the body, and that one is actually eternal and deathless—a realization that automatically lessens or even dissolves the fear of dying that can be crippling for many.

(It's also believed in the yogic tradition that one leaves the physical body every night when falling asleep; however the difference between this and formal astral projection is that dreaming is not ordinarily a conscious projection out of the body. But a "back door" way of developing astral projection is through lucid dreaming, where one becomes conscious while still in the dream state, and in turn more conversant in the ways of the astral world that one will also encounter upon physical death.)

Lastly, Kriyananda emphasized the value of developing a personal relationship with one's chosen deity, in Hinduism referred to as the Ishta Devata—*whether that be Jesus, Buddha, Krishna, Mary, Quan Yin, or some other divine personage. While fully recognizing that "God" can't be limited to a specific form, mystics have long recognized the usefulness of employing a form or symbol in helping to develop a meditative relationship with the formless. In so doing, one ideally becomes on such intimate terms with one's Ishta Devata that one is able to converse with it much like one would a close friend. This not only helps to open up the channels of consciousness to one's own higher nature, but enables one on death to more easily establish a connection with that luminous sense of divinity which appears upon crossing over.*

In a small pamphlet titled Kriya Bindu, Kriyananda wrote: "The most vital task for all Kriya Yogis is to have a complete understanding of the birth-death-rebirth cycle. When you find Self-Conscious Awareness in the midst of the birth-death-rebirth cycle, you no longer see or perceive birth or death as does the ordinary earthling. At this moment you will understand that birth and death are Samadhi. Thus the desire to escape birth and death ceases. Thus you are free from the suffering of death as well as life. This is the key fundamental principle of Kriya Yoga. *This principle transcends all other principles."* (Italics Kriyananda's)

During the stages of sleep, dreaming and waking, the silver cord that connects our physical body with the astral body remains unbroken, so that we're still able to move through the tunnel back into the physical mind-body complex. That cord connects the Ajna chakra or "third eye" (which is gold in color and located between the eyebrows of the physical body) with the Chandra chakra (which is silver and located at the base of the skull of the astral body). With the death of the physical body, however, the silver cord that connects the physical and astral bodies is damaged and thus we cannot re-enter the physical body through this tunnel.

When you die, there will be a person waiting for you. It may be a relative, guru or religious figure, or a "guide" that will help you, or at least fill you in on your predicament. If you are a disciple in the Kriya lineage, or a close student in any spiritual lineage for that matter, when you die there will most likely be one or all of your lineage standing there to guide you.

At some point in the death and dying process, the soul passes from the physical realm into the astral realm by moving through a tunnel of light, which has three sections, each section being larger than the previous one. The first section is colored yellow, the next is blue and the last one is white. The yellow zone indicates the astral world, where most people go and then are forced to return to the earth plane because of their karma. The blue zone is the causal world, where a few souls stay in-between incarnations and then choose to return to the earth plane to help humans mature and evolve. The white zone is the divine zone, in which souls who exist here generally do not choose to return to the earth plane, or they may choose to descend into the lower two zones—the astral and causal—and help beings who reside there.

As the soul moves through this tunnel, it senses other souls--some moving in the same direction, others moving in the opposite direction. (Notice the similarity here with the Old Testament story of "Jacob's ladder" - RG.) On the left side there is a cool, snowy path. On the right side there is a warm, dry path. Most people take the dry, warm path. However, the yogis say to take the cool, snowy path if you wish to speed up your evolution. On both sides you will meet some of your closer relatives and friends who are there to greet and help you. On the 18th day after death, you can choose to stay within the force-field of the earth or pass through it, and enter the blue zone. Almost all souls remain in the yellow zone level and later reincarnate back on one of the earth planes.

It is important to keep a peaceful and focused mind during the progression of the death process so that your mind can be in complete attunement to Life's goodness and to the Infinite. It is at this moment that all the yoga you practiced while on earth will truly be rewarded. Self-mastery must manifest at this moment if you wish to soften the karma of your past earth life and speed up your spiritual evolution. You can develop this mastery by daily meditating, by turning within and upward to observe the mind.

In so doing, you learn to control the mind. Daily practice will give you the ability to discern what is happening in the depths of your soul, giving you the power to focus on what you choose, not simply on what the mind's karma desires. Invoking a divine name or calling upon your guru are ways you can link to the Infinite and connect more fully with the divine mind, and also helps to lift you to a higher astral spiritual level. Chanting a mantra is an excellent means to break through obstructions and evoke freedom within your soul.

The death process is complete when the mind state leaves the physical body. For the ordinary person this leads to a state of semiconsciousness much like that of sleep, during which there may be a fleeting glimmer of awareness such as also occurs while dreaming. Mystics, yogis and deep meditators, however, remain conscious and are more fully aware of life on the "other side."

According to yoga there is no need to be fearful of death because almost everyone continues doing in the death state what they did while on the earth. A shoemaker continues to make shoes, a housewife continues to do housework, a soldier continues to soldier. Death is largely an extension of your earth life. In short, there is only life. Live it and find joy. Find joy here and now and you will have joy in the astral.

Then, after a period of doing on the astral what one did on earth, that consciousness fades away and the mind goes through a transformation in which the strongest desire one had on earth starts to manifest. For example, if the housewife's deep desire was to become a doctor, she would become a doctor in the astral world in order to balance out her desire energy. However, if that astral experience does not satisfy her emotional need, she will then become a doctor when she reincarnates on earth.

Depending on what part of the astral world you wind up in, your astral body generally looks like it did in the prime of your earth life. Your astral body is as real and feels as solid as the one you now inhabit. You will still have your five senses because in truth your physical, sensory and intellectual abilities are an extension of the very same sensory powers that function in your subtle body. Furthermore, when you no longer inhabit your physical body, all your senses function better than when you are embodied because there are no physical bodily distractions.

In the astral realm beyond death, time is essentially reversed from how you experience it here. You grow progressively younger there rather than older, like here.

In preparing to be reborn, the soul must find a female body to inhabit so as to fulfill its karma, and in turn a father whose karma matches that of the mother. But the karma of both parents must suit that of the incoming soul. For example, if the child is destined be the first person to walk on the Moon, then the mother's and the father's karma must be to have a child who will be the first person on the Moon. Or, if the child is to die at the age of three, the parents must have the karma to lose a child at the age of three. In short, the karma of the three persons must merge and match.

※※

Often a child dies before being physically born, whether through miscarriage or abortion. However, even if the child lives in the womb for only one month, it still has had a very meaningful experience, during which time the mother and the child have loved, shared and experienced much together by neutralizing karma and speeding up the mother's evolution.

※※

In short, there is no life and death, there is only *consciousness* and *unconsciousness*—scattered awareness and focused awareness.

PART III
THE CONVERSATIONS

As mentioned earlier, Kriyananda was always generous with his time in speaking with me. Our conversations covered a wide range of topics, from the down-to-earth to the philosophical, from the trivial to the profound. Most of our exchanges were not recorded and generally took place between lectures when I would walk into his office to ask questions; yet there were many occasions when I was able to sit with him for an hour or more and pitch questions to him. Some of those were recorded, and it's from that batch of recordings that I've selected out a small sampling of exchanges, as a cross-section of our interactions. The earliest of these dates back to 1976 while the latest was recorded in 1983.

RAY: You mentioned once how a big part of the reason you respected Shelly so much was his ability to balance out his mystical life with his everyday life, and that not many people seemed able to do that.

KRIYANANDA: That's right.

RAY: Why is that such a difficult balancing act?

KRIYANANDA: I think it's because, in a sense, most of us in the spiritual world are introverted, we're artistic, we're withdrawn, we are not by nature aggressive or practical. And then there's the rest of humanity—probably the vast majority of us, in fact—who are aggressive, assertive, materialistic, and have little or no sensitivity.

And once you find the soul who has pretty well brought the two together into a balance, where neither one really predominates, you have truly found what I would call an enlightened soul. As opposed to the so-called "saints" who flounder around and get spacey for months at a time, or who become unconscious for weeks on end and are just out of balance. The ability to deal with this world as well as the astral and spiritual worlds is one of the the great proofs of spiritual growth.

Now, some of us can do a hell of a good job of dealing just with this world, which I still consider to be a spiritual victory, I genuinely do. It's one of the reasons I've always had a certain respect for successful businessmen. That's assuming that what they're doing is being done volitionally and by conscious effort, and not just by a lot of good karma from the past. But even so, at one point that took a lot of effort. But you've got to balance that worldly ability with the ability to walk through the dream state or the mystical state consciously. That's definitely a mark of an enlightened soul.

RAY: What is the difference between someone who feels guided by *destiny* versus someone who is simply being pushed by *desire*?

KRIYANANDA: Well, I could get nasty here and say I think they're actually one and the same. Now, I know that's not completely true, but for the average person, 99% of the time those two things are probably identical. I think that the feeling one is being "guided by destiny" is really just a very intense desire being camouflaged in a cloak of respectability.

RAY: I think I understand what you mean. Hitler or Mussolini no doubt felt they were being "guided by destiny," but look at what they did.

KRIYANANDA: That's right. To put it in plain English, if someone says that say that they *think* they are being guided by destiny, then I'd say it's the same thing. But if you say that a person *knows* he's being guided by destiny, then that's a different awareness.

RAY: Is there any way of telling all of these different shades within a horoscope?

KRIYANANDA: Yes. I would tend to feel that a person who is guided by destiny would probably have two very complex patterns. I would think that their Sun would be trine to the Neptune, while at the same time Neptune is squaring or opposing the Moon. Or I would think that the Mercury might be conjunct Jupiter and trining out Saturn. Something of this nature.

RAY: So what do you think destiny actually *is*, then?

KRIYANANDA: (Pause) Destiny is an awareness that there are forces acting in the universe which are precipitating events, and the individual says, "These forces must crystallize at this time and space and causation, and I am wiling to help the crystallization."

RAY: Do you feel the 10th house or the Midheaven is somehow linked to that sense of destiny?

KRIYANANDA: Yeah, I suppose it's basically because that's the highest point in the chart (or the "lowest" point within the chart, technically speaking). Or perhaps it's because that point is related to Saturn, which is the principle of crystallization, and so ultimately relates to everything coming to a summation, an ending point, which is a final crystallization. And therefore we call that final crystallization "destiny," or the future, because it stands out as most crystallized.

Another area of difference between Kriyananda and Shelly was in their respective attitudes towards the arts. Whereas Shelly had great respect for artists, Kriyananda tended to feel art was comparatively unimportant in the larger scheme of things. While he respected talent, he didn't see it as a substitute for spiritual discipline or higher insights, let alone a compassionate heart. That perspective comes through loud and clear in this exchange.

RAY: Why is it so many of the truly creative people I've encountered don't seem very "aware"? I mean that in terms of seeming pretty insensitive about other people, or even being unconscious of themselves, their motives, actions, and so on.

KRIYANANDA: (Pause) I think that really creative people are often not very aware because their minds are so focused on their creativity, rather than that what is around them. Creativity by its very nature is very *focussed*. Part of the process of creativity is focusing on what you are trying to create. And so, they're usually *not* very aware because they're lost in the creativity, and that pattern of creativity.

RAY: But yogis are very focussed in their respective area, too, so why are *they* relatively aware? Why are they not similarly *unaware*?

KRIYANANDA: Because most creativity, for the average human being, comes about because of a concentration, which is a constriction of the mind-stuff, a focusing. Whereas most yogis, choose the opposite direction, which is more of a meditative approach, and therefore have a larger horizon of awareness.

RAY: Interesting.

KRIYANANDA: Also, creative people tend to think that art is everything. It's all there really is! Whereas the yogi thinks, art is nothing—compared to God, that is. Their focus is more galactic. I think that's very important.

RAY: But art, as a Venusian thing, is a heart-chakra matter, so I've always thought it could be a liberating force. Or is it just an entrapment?

KRIYANANDA: (Pause) I think it's an entrapment, I really do. Now, that doesn't mean I'm right!

RAY: But it can inspire!

KRIYANANDA: To do what, though? You know, there's the old question: what is art? I belong to the old Greek school—about the only Greek school of thought I resonate to, actually—which says: *art is art, but only if it's didactic.* You know what I'm saying? There's a *message* to it. But I'm afraid that so much of what we call art...

RAY: ...is just entertainment?

KRIYANANDA: It's just entertainment. That really isn't "art," in my opinion. And therefore I would take the more "Venusian" approach as being....an entrapment, really. And a potentially very dangerous entrapment.

RAY: Do you feel that music is any more or less of an entrapment? It's more "Neptunian" or ethereal, and the fact that it's less tangible seems to take one deeper somehow...

KRIYANANDA: I think it has a deeper level *meaning*...... And yet music is the thing that armies are built upon.

RAY: It can be very manipulative, I know, even more than the visual arts, in some ways.

KRIYANANDA: Very much so.

RAY: But what about that level, where you can see a painting and it might have no didactic meaning, but it's so beautiful that it inspires you, it stirs something in your soul. What about the value there?

KRIYANANDA: Well, the value there is that it's a *mirror*. In and of itself. But what if the inspiration is to conquer the world?

RAY: Hmm....Let me think about that.

One of the more thought-provoking comments Goswami Kriyananda made during our communications, and one that's easily misunderstood as being pessimistic, took place during a time when I was researching the topic of "invisible beings"—ghosts, discarnate souls, guides, angels, etc. I emailed him this question, and his response was surprisingly brief.

RAY: Are there disembodied beings around us all the time, as some claim, which are simply invisible to the naked eye?

His simple response: "You are alone in your universe."

There are several ways to interpret that answer, but I think it's important to note that Kriyananda specifically said "your" universe there, not "the" universe. But I'm also reminded of a comment cited earlier in these pages: "You can look down from the vantage point of the Ajna chakra and see everybody else's material and mental realms. You see an infinite number of sidereal universes, and surrounding each spark of God is built a universe."

RAY: What is humor? When someone laughs, what is the mystical mechanism going on there?

KRIYANANDA: Simply put, the mystical "mechanism" of humor is generally to put something out of place. Seeing anything out of place is humorous. A man slipping on a banana peel and landing on his rear can be funny, because we all know that the right place for a man is on the soles of his feet, not on his rear. And so the essence of mysticism is to point out, intellectually or Zen-wise, the ridiculous situation where we are at. We're not where we're supposed to be, and that is funny. And so we talk about the cosmic humor of God, you know. If that's the question you're asking.

RAY: It is, in a way. But I'm curious, when we laugh what is actually happening in our soul, psychically, energetically?

KRIYANANDA: When you laugh, *you break loose of any attachment.* There's a momentary abatement of the confusion of the experiencer with the experience. The mind may go and grab it back again, but for a moment the attachment is broken. Someone comes into the room and threatens to shoot another person, that's not funny at all. But suppose the person who's being threatened, his pants unexpectedly fall down. And the guy with the gun goes, "Ha ha!" It might get all serious again, of course, but momentarily at least the energy is broken. And the guy who lost his pants is probably going to survive, more often than not, because the shooter broke free from that man's karma, as a result of that humor. So humor breaks loose from both sides.

Similar to Yogananda, Kriyananda sometimes hinted at having had past lives in the military. For example, Yogananda spoke openly about his belief that he had been William the Conqueror, who stormed the beaches of England in 1066. Kriyananda once alluded (indirectly) to having been a Mexican freedom-fighter in his most recent life. I initially found these accounts odd, and asked him to explain that seeming incongruity, between militaristic impulses in one life and more "spiritual" ones in another.

Ray: I'm not sure I understand how such a formidable spiritual teacher as Yogananda might have had recent past lives in the military, and on the battlefield. There seems to be something incongruous about that, since it's such an abrupt change, from something relatively violent to something more benevolent and mystical.

KRIYANANDA: Ahhh...You see, there's more of the general in the guru than you think, and more of the guru in the general! (Laughs)

That last comment reminded me of something I read about in an article about the American wartime figure, General Patton, who spoke openly of having experienced combat in previous lives, including as a Roman legionnaire. Before the 1943 invasion of Sicily, British General Harold Alexander told Patton, "You know, George, you would have made a great marshal for Napoleon if you had lived in the 19th century." Patton replied, "But I did." Patton believed that after he died he would return to once again lead armies into battle.

―――

RAY: What is the most important thing you can say to someone who is suffering, who is dealing with adversity?

KRIYANANDA: (Pause) The most important thing is to realize there are people who are in far worse situations than yourself. As painful as your situation may be, it really is as nothing compared to what some others in the world are dealing with. That is the starting point.

―――

RAY: You once spoke about men having the souls of women, and women having the souls of men. I never really understood what that meant. If you have the soul of a woman, why aren't you a woman then?

KRIYANNDA: But you *are*—subconsciously.

RAY: How come we don't act like it, though?

KRIYANANDA: But you do. As I've come to understand it, in terms of reincarnation we incarnate as a man, then as a woman, then as a man, and so on—though it may not always be quite so regular as that, from one lifetime directly to the next. But that male/female switch gives us a bi-focal understanding, psychically, so that we are able to get what I call a depth perception of life, not what 'man' is or not what 'woman' is, exclusively. So if I am over here as a man, I know that eventually it will be over there, that already my subconscious is swinging in this direction, towards femininity.

It sort of comes back to Jung's notion, with his anima/animus idea, that the subconscious mind is the opposite polarity. Actually, that's part of the reason why men call the ships they build "she," and never "he." However, if women were to build ships, they would definitely call them "he"! There's a great secret there about life.

RAY: Why is it that the kindest, most compassionate people I've met tend to be the ones with the difficult horoscopes, with the most painful karmas?

KRIYANANDA: Yeah, that's almost always true.

RAY: But why?

KRIYANANDA: Because the people who have the worst aspects, tons of squares and oppositions, are people who have suffered a great deal. And people who have suffered a great deal are usually very kind people. You see, one of the mistakes that many modern astrologers make is they believe that squares or oppositions are due to "bad karma." And they're not. Many times we induce difficult squares into a chart when we're born in order to accomplish something. One of the most common examples of that is, look for someone who has four or five or six squares to Pluto, and you will find someone who is extremely concerned about mankind as a race. Not just two or three people, but mankind as a race. He or she will have a lot of pain, a lot of suffering and anguish, and the square will manifest, but it will also tend to give them enough energy to accomplish or override the chart, enough energy to do what has to be done. But those sorts of people usually have a lot of deep feelings; a lot of squares bring a lot of sensitivity, both good *and* bad. It's the people who have nothing but sextiles and trines who are usually incredibly indifferent.

RAY: You made an interesting comment the other day how if you want to know something about someone's Martian (i.e., third, "Manipura") chakra, look to their attitudes towards war, or sports.

KRIYANANDA: Right. One's attitude towards war or sports says something about the Martian chakra, and that in turn reveals how much energy one has, or one's physical resilience, as well as one's attitude towards life generally, in terms of the struggle of it all.

RAY: That's fascinating. I'm curious about the other chakras. Are there any things in particular you would say along those same lines, as far as any similar symbolic "indexes" for those?

KRIYANANDA: How about fruit and Jupiter? One's attitude towards fruit would indicate one's lust for life in a positive sense, or one's enthusiasm for life, if you prefer. Or one's attitudes towards books would indicate something about your throat chakra and your intellectual capacity, and your openness to knowledge. Every chakra has its own set of symbolic correspondences like that, so it's fairly simple to go through and see what types of connections that reveals. You learn a great deal about your inner, occult psychology by your attitudes towards things in the world around you.

RAY: When I'm in a jet and flying through clouds, something about that imagery outside the window has a profound impact on me, and feels strangely familiar, almost like it's "home." Is that a memory from some distant past experience?

KRIYANANDA: Yes, there are three reasons that it's moving for you. One is, it is definitely an intense memory of astral flight. Secondly, it reminds us of our dream state, and so it lifts us into what I call the lower astral by association. Because in the lower astral we fly a great deal. And third, it is triggering your Mercury. So in connection with your Mercury—whether by house, sign, aspects, declinations or otherwise—there will be some favorable creative patterning that's being triggered.

RAY: Mercury...?

KRIYANANDA: The ritual of flying, the very act of flying will stimulate your Mercury. And so if you've got a good Mercury, flying will trigger more positive feelings. If you've got a very difficult Mercury, well, not so much.

RAY: It's hard for me to describe how deeply the imagery of those clouds affects me sometimes. I wonder if those cloud formations may be reminiscent of actual astral structures, perhaps?

KRIYANANDA: The inner planes are cloudy, cloud-filled. That's partly why we say that heaven is up. It's definitely a memory track for you, just as it is for me. Remember, clouds are always the symbol of purity. Not necessarily moral purity, but...

RAY: Even storm clouds, or thunderheads?

KRIYANANDA: I believe they still are. The thunderhead reflects a cleansing process, a catharsis. But it's definitely a cleansing, a purification of the air. For me, though, the key trigger symbol has always been snowflakes. I'm snowflake oriented.

RAY: Why is that?

KRIYANANDA: It's a Neptunian force in my chart. And so whenever it snows—even just thinking about it now triggers a very intense memory track for me, an emotional pattern. Each person is different. For some people it's mud, for some people its green grass, for some people its flowers. But for me, it's snow. (Kriyananda often cited a verse from the 15th Century French poet Francois Villon in his lectures: "Where or where are the snows of yesteryear?" - RG)

RAY: During the astrology workshop you delivered on karmic astrology up in Michigan, why did you say you felt that Saturn trine Venus was the "most spiritual aspect," or at least one of the more spiritual aspects a person can have in their horoscope?

KRIYANANDA: Because Venus, in the sense that we were talking about in more occult terms, represents the heart chakra; it is love as humans understand it. And Saturn is the ability to lock in harmoniously and not to forget that love. Saturn trine Venus not only shows that one has loved in one's past, but that one has consciously locked that piece of karma into a permanent facet so that one can remember what it really was. You have a reference point to measure everything else. I believe I followed that statement of mine you're referring to about Saturn-trine-Venus with,

"...particularly if it comes out of a fixed sign." All that means is that one now has a measuring stick by which to measure everything. Saturn trine Venus shows that one remembers what love is, and therefore one isn't going to be easily deceived by greed or by sexuality or by words.

RAY: Then what about Saturn *square* Venus? What does that show?

KRIYANANDA: Generally? It tends to indicate selfishness. Like I say, *tends*. The person may find it very hard to remember what real love is like, and maybe be turned completely off to the possibility that it even exists, thinking "There is no such thing."

RAY: And yet I have seen great artists with that aspect.

KRIYANANDA: But great artists aren't necessarily spiritual. Great artists are often "sex-ers," they take their sexual energies and their enthusiasm about a new partner, and transfer it into art. Which is why so much of the history of Western music and art has been as decadent as it's been, spiritually speaking.

RAY: But isn't creativity rooted in something divine, something spiritual?

KRIYANANDA: Well, in Christian culture we tend to equate creativity with godliness, but that's just not always the case. That's why good old "black magicians" can be helpful reminders to have around, since they are individuals with that ability to create and yet can be bad guys.

RG: But it seems to me those gifted with great creative abilities, whether that be Beethoven or Bach or even black magicians, have the *potential* for spiritual greatness, no?

KRIYANANDA: They do. But you see, all they're doing is working out of the 11th house, of aspirations, and not linked to the other three fixed signs. They're incomplete. It's called selfishness.

RAY: If you had to leave just one simple teaching behind for your students to contemplate after you're gone, what would it be?

KRIYANANDA: (Long pause) Enjoy life. We're not here to suffer, but to learn, and to enjoy this garden of God. Find joy in whatever you do.

RAY: What's the difference between "spirit" and "soul"?

KRIYANANDA: You can think of spirit as the core awareness, the I AM principle, whereas "soul" is the memory track, the sheath of stored experiences that spirit accumulates over time.

RAY: Would it be safe to say that spirit is what you *are*, but soul is something you *have*?

KRIYANANDA: Yes, I think that's acceptable.

The following exchange wasn't recorded, but what I relate here comes as close as I can recall to what was said.

RAY: Mystic and occultists often talk about the "akashic records," which are sometimes described as the records in the ethers of all that has ever happened. But you also said something about how we can learn about the future there as well. Could you elaborate on that a bit?

KRIYANANDA: Okay. In the higher levels of the astral plane—the Mercury sub-plane of the fifth Mercury plane, to be specific—there is a room of books, or what the mind perceives to be a room of books. There are twelve volumes there, and they're written in the language of symbols. But the eleventh volume there concerns the future of what is yet to come. What's interesting is that when you open it up to the last page in that volume, you'll see that it's blank. But there will be writing taking form on the page right before your eyes, then when that page fills up, you turn it—and a new blank page appears. In other words, the future is never completely written, but is always in a state of becoming.

Here is another exchange that wasn't recorded, this from a gathering my friend Dave Blair assembled during the 1980s. Kriyananda's answer was a lengthy and highly personal one; unfortunately, the only part of his answer I clearly recall now was his opening comment, but I felt that was worth sharing since it touched on a struggle experienced by many others.

RAY: If it's not too personal, what was your greatest challenge when you first began walking the spiritual path?

KRIYANANDA: (Long pause) Self-acceptance. It took me a long time to learn to accept myself, and my many limitations.

RAY: Esoterically speaking, what is "imagination"?

KRIYANANDA: I feel imagination is nothing but memory. Anything you can imagine, or think you can imagine, consciously or unconsciously, is but a memory track from the past, on this plane or on other planes, astral or otherwise.

RAY: I once heard you suggest that difficult or destructive patterns in the horoscope are sometimes really just memory imprints from the past that we have a hard time breaking free of. What did you mean?

KRIYANANDA: Suppose that someone was born with Saturn square to their Sun, which may indicate they were abused by a parent or someone in authority in a past life. So they come into this world with that imprint, that memory, and come to expect this will continue to happen and that all authority figures are bastards. And what usually occurs in those cases is that whenever that pattern is triggered by some transit or progression, their subconscious mind will in its ignorance tend to fill in those aspects with the appropriate event, which will usually be an unpleasant one involving authorities of some sort.

RAY: So how does one learn to break that pattern, that memory imprint?

KRIYANANDA: Okay. Suppose you could hold to a positive thought when that "bad aspect" fires, instead of responding negatively or karmically. If you can do that, you won't allow the subconscious mind to suck in the negative event through that now-present "gap," which you can think of as a sort of valve in consciousness that opens up to leak out some of the ripened karma.

Or perhaps the difficult triggering event will still come in, but you've corrected your attitude so the event doesn't really affect you. You know, the boss might say, "Damn it, get your ass in here, Joe," which triggers all of those latent hatreds and abuses, all those negative memory imprints. The natural reaction in those situations of course is to throw a book at him, or shoot him, or just leave work. And you quit your job and the wife gets a divorce because you're not caring for the children, and the children go out and rob because they have no father, and so on—you know, the whole chain of events.

But the other option here would be to balance yourself and instead say something to the boss like, "Yes sir, I'm sorry." You're standing at attention, you're being humble, and you eat humble pie, and you understand that he's doing his job so you tell him how much you appreciate his work—and the next thing you know, you've got a promotion. You see, it's all about attitude, and for most people that's based on a memory.

RAY: In a recent class you mentioned how certain karmic lessons extend over multiple lifetimes, and how these can "peak" at some point almost like the rising and falling of a wave. You then suggested the horoscope can actually give clues as to where that karma is in that sequence, in terms of whether it's waxing or waning. What were you referring to?

KRIYANANDA: Yes, let's say a person has a Mars-square-Venus in their horoscope, which shows, in simple terms, they're dealing with karmic lessons relating to love and relationships, maybe to sexuality or even money. If the aspect is approaching (which means that the faster-moving planet is in a lower degree than the slower-moving planet), that indicates that lesson has not yet completed, and that if it isn't learned in this lifetime it will finish up in some future lifetime. In short, it shows they have more work to do in that area.

RAY: So what if the aspect is separating (where the faster-moving planet is a higher degree than the slower-moving one)?

KRIYANDANDA: Then it's a lesson they've essentially learned, or maybe even resolved and mastered, but it still plays an important role in the experiences of this incarnation, especially if the aspect is close.

RAY: Then what if the aspect is exact, and those two planets are in the same exact degree of their respective signs?

KRIYANANDA: Then that means this particular lifetime is "ground zero" for that lesson, as it were. I would pay particular attention to any aspect that's exact, whether it's positive or negative, because it shows something that is a central concern or lesson for this specific incarnation. The closer the aspect is, the more important the role it plays in this life.

RAY: Personally, I can't see auras, but let's say you're looking at auras. What colors in a person's aura would relate to which planets or principles, exactly?

KRIYANANDA: I'll talk in general terms here. Usually, Saturn relates to black, and to very dark colors. Occasionally that brings in some of the darker muddier browns, but not everyone thinks that. Mars relates to red, or again, occasionally brown coloration—"earth tones" is what they call them. Venus relates to green colors. Mercury relates to violets and magenta.

RAY: Does purple relate to Jupiter?

KRIYANANDA: Yeah, that's Jupiter.

RAY: What would show a heavily "lunar" person, someone under the influence of the Moon?

KRIYANANDA: That would be milk-white.

RAY: What about a heavily "solar" person?

KRIYANANDA: That would be the orange-yellows.

RAY: What about a flaming white aura on someone?

KRIYANANDA: There's no such thing.

RAY: There's no such thing?

KRIYANANDA: No, there isn't. Now, there can be a *flaming colorless* aura, but that's not the same.

RAY: That would relate to a higher kind of samadhic awareness?

KRIYANANDA: Yes.

RAY: So would that relate to the Sun, or to a pronounced Sun center, Ajna chakra (the Third Eye)?

KRIYANANDA: The Ajna chakra energy would be either a golden yellow or gold.

RAY: Shelly talks about our having come into God's cosmic dream from the "outside," and learning from his pathways in here. But you said something recently to the effect that the fact we even entered into God's cosmic dream in the first place implies we were "already illuminated," in a sense. Could you elaborate on that a bit?

KRIYANANDA: Yes, there's the implication that to realize there is even such a thing as "God's dream," and to even conceive of the thought, "I want to enter this dream," mystically at least implies you're already there, and that all you're really changing is the intensity of the dream.

RAY: But that leads me to ask, why even enter into that cosmic dream if you're already there?

KRIYANANDA: I'll put it like this. It's like smelling the food from the kitchen—that's the example Shelly gave me. And if the food smells that good, imagine how much better it would *actually taste*. You see? Other people might approach it differently. To be able to enter into the dream of God means that you then stand to gain the yoga siddhis, the divine energies and powers associated with living in that dream—and therefore you can heal people, you can help people.

Or to put it even more mystically, by entering in that cosmic dream you can then *help God* with his responsibility. If you're not wealthy, it's pretty hard to build a hospital for somebody. But if you're wealthy, it's a little easier to build the hospital. So if you pick up the spiritual energies or the spiritual powers—which is a word I don't really like, to be honest—then from that particular standpoint you can help God more because now you have the health, the money, the power, whatever word you want to use, to accomplish what needs to be accomplished. Presuming you have the wisdom to know what needs to be done, that is.

But if someone ways, "There is no God, it's all a bunch of hokum, there's nothing here but this goddamn world!"—they're basically so far removed from the dream of God in their awareness that they could never even enter into it, because they're not even aware it's there. So to be *aware* it's there, regardless of how they got that initial awareness, is really *being* there. To conceive it is really to have it. The only difference now is, you actually have it, you want it, more abundantly, more fully, more completely. We call it the intensification, or the recycling, or as Shelly would call it, the "retracking" of the energies.

RAY: You've said that our different emotional or psychological states are related to how our energies are configured within our various chakras, and within the three channels of energy along and around the spine—Ida, Pingala, and Sushumna.

KRIYANANDA: That's right.

RAY: So what exactly is the difference between the types of mental or emotional states in those two peripheral channels of Ida and Pingala, as opposed to what we experience in Sushumna?

KRIYANANDA: Well, in the very simplest of terms, you could say that that middle channel is associated with *feelings*, but once the energy drops out of that middle channel, out of Sushumna, they are no longer *feelings* and they become *emotions*—and there is a difference. As emotions, they're more compulsive and can be either constructive or destructive. Even when we talk about logic, which is more on the right-hand side, you still have that duality of good or bad, constructive or destructive. So the outer channels that exist along the right and left-hand side of the spine are very dualistic.

RAY: Can a person experience emotions that are so subtle that they *seem* like feelings? Like when I see a sad movie and it causes me to experience deep emotions? They may not compel me to do anything, but is it really just a shallow sentimentality? Or can it extend deeper than that? How can one really tell the difference?

KRIYANANDA: I asked Shelly once, How do you really know that you're awake? He said to me it's basically just a question of self-awareness, that you *know* it simply through self-awareness. And I said, "Aw, Shelly, that's a terrible answer!" Yep—but it's the answer! You know it, really, by knowing it in a deeper way, through refining your perception and coming to a point where you see an emotion and you say, "Ah! This is a gross emotion! And that over there is a subtle emotion—but it's still an emotion."

RAY: Okay, now you and Shelly explain that Sushumna is the state of balanced consciousness associated with the middle of the spine, the central "pillar." But how does Sushumna at the root chakra level differ from Sushumna at the heart chakra level? Are there differences in the experience of Sushumna at the different levels, or is it the same all the way up?

KRIYANANDA: There are finer degrees, finer balances, levels of balance within balance, you could say. How about this: have you ever played with one of these toy tops, the gyroscope kind that you spin out onto the table or the floor? And you know about those large gyroscopes in places like Boulder Dam, right? Sushumna is a theoretical point of balance, and they're all the same, in a sense, but there's a difference between a top running and tipping over and going against the wall, and a large gyro getting out of balance and ripping loose from the generator

RAY: Oh, So you're saying the latter one is more Saturnian, more like the root chakra kind of Sushumna?

KRIYANANDA: That's right, that's the only difference. And it can be more destructive, in terms of physical consequences.

RAY: You and Shelly talk a great deal about how the different visible planets relate to the different chakras, symbolically. Saturn is related to the root chakra, Jupiter to the second chakra, and so on, on up to the Sun and Moon, those centers within the head. But what about Uranus, Neptune and Pluto? Do they relate to other chakras, or to chakras that exist lower down on the spine below the root chakra?

KRIYANANDA: No, there are no "pre-Saturnian chakras" in that sense, if that's what you mean. Those outer planets relate to the existing chakras like this: Every chakra has two planetary rulers, as well as two zodiacal signs. For example, the root chakra is associated with both Capricorn and Aquarius, and with the planets Saturn/Uranus. Now, the planet that is superior to the sister or brother planet, will tell you as best as possible what the chakra quality is about. In the case of the root chakra, for instance, Saturn is probably *closer* to expressing the meaning of that level.

But beyond those two planets, and the *blending* of the two planets, there is something which I suppose we could call the "bindu" of the chakra, the very center point of the chakra, within the central Sushumnic channel. That's a third point, and it's perhaps the most important aspect of the chakra.

RAY: Does that have any symbolic representation within the astrological system?

KRIYANANDA: No, it has no representation in terms of any planetary symbol, and that's because it is *unmanifested*.

RAY: I was wondering if you could talk to me about contacting higher beings or spirits in the dream state, as a way of acquiring knowledge?

KRIYANANDA: Okay. There are a few different approaches to gathering metaphysical knowledge in that way. The old Jewish/Babylonian/Chaldean/Egyptian system primarily utilized ceremonies to invoke non-physical beings—some called them "demons," but "elementals" is probably a better words to use.

RAY: "Demons" meaning what?

KRIYANANDA: "Demons" meaning *beings who are below us*. But "elementals" is probably a better word to use. Trouble is, human beings are not very capable of distinguishing between the elementals and the demons. We do not have enough sensitivity to determine when we draw an elemental into our life whether it is truly an elemental—which is neither good nor bad—or is a lower vibrational entity, which in our language is "demonic." Which really means that—like us, ha!—they're more selfish and more self-destructive to us.

There are areas of the world where you can conduct rituals for establishing patterns of attaining angels. I'm frankly not sure they really are "angels," to be honest, but they are certainly entities that are much more harmonious and positive to us. And these entities can transfer enormous amounts of information to you.

RAY: Now, as for this transfer of information...do these entities come to you in dreams?

KRIYANANDA: In the dream state, or if you're highly sensitive, they will come to you in a trance state. There are very intricate rituals for going about this, and then there are relatively simple procedures.

RAY: Why don't we start with the simpler ones for now, and if we have more time at a later time, we can go into the more complex ones, okay?

KRIYANANDA: Okay. You can just give a name to one of these higher entities—you can look up a name, and whatever the name might be, say, "Come to me in the dream state, come to me in the dream state..." And that act of invoking, that chant or that mantra, whether it's nonsensical or otherwise, is simply saying, "Come to me in the dream and teach me about such-and-such"—and fill in the blank. It could be European history, American history, my ancestry, or you know, the end of the world—whatever it may be. That's all. That's a very, very simple way of doing it. And relatively harmless.

RAY: Is the mantra or the chanting part of it essential?

KRIYANANDA: It probably would help, and some would say that yes, it's essential. In my opinion you can use English; it would probably be better to use English, symbolically. But whatever you consider an "angel" to be; give it a symbol, a name. "Oh, you phantoms of the deeper mind that transcend time and space, come forth from the planes where thou exist, come forth into my dream state. Teach me, oh thou great ones about such-and-such." Whatever the name, just fill it in. This is usually done for about 45 minutes to an hour, on every New Moon, and occasionally on every Full Moon. And you just run with that until it manifests.

RAY: Do you mean doing it just once during that one period, then the next period?

KRIYANANDA: You can do it every night, but usually, historically, it is done every new moon, every full moon, every new moon, every full moon...until the entity appears. And it will appear in a form.

Once it gets into a form, keep asking yourself, *What is thy magical name?* You mentally say this, alright? So when this entity appears—and you'll know when it appears that it's not a dream entity and is one that you've either created or drawn in from another space-time continuum—then you must ask, *What's your magical name?* And as soon as he gives you its name, then by calling that name it's supposed to respond to you, whether you actually see it or not.

RAY: I'm frankly a bit concerned about drawing in the wrong beings, perhaps "lower" entities. I wouldn't want to contact anything that is, well, questionable.

KRIYANANDA: No, these are higher beings. You know, *you can only draw in the higher realm beings relative to your degree of purity.* That's why extensive purifications are emphasized so strongly with these procedures.

Here's an analogy to help explain that. It's like waking up to your partner but he or she smells like they've been sleeping in their clothes for years, and never taken a bath. It'd be pretty hard to make love or even get near them, if you'll permit me. In the same way, your bodily desires create an incense that can be offensive to the higher angels—"desire incense," as it's called—so that they can't come near even if they want to. They have no way of holding their noses! (laughs). So that's the secret. You can have *intent*, but you should not have *desire* in these procedures.

RAY: "You can only draw in the higher realm being that's relative to your degree of purity." That's very interesting.

KRIYANANDA: You draw in whatever you're relative to. Now, there's another method that is even simpler than that one. Think of all the dead saints and sages of all the world's religions, and from all of them pick out the one you feel is closest to you, in terms of the highest and most idealistic and that you resonate with. Okay?

Let's say it's Sri Aurobindo, just as an example. Whether you want to call him Sri Aurobindo, Sri Ji, Bindo, or whatever you want to call him, try to get onto a relatively intimate level with him, as it were—take their name and modify it as needed, similar to the way you might speak to someone named Thomas as "Tommy." For instance, suppose you were Sri Aurobindo's older brother or father or friend, would you walk up to him and say, "*Sri Aurobindo Ji*"? No, you wouldn't. You would call him Goshi, or something like that. Nothing disrespectful, of course, but you have to come up with an intimate name, and generate that in your imagination.

And then, day and night, either out loud or silent, you say (for example), "Bindo, come to me in my dreams, Bindo, come to me in my dreams"—and so on, over and over, continuously. Okay? And then each night you say, "I wonder if he'll come tonight?" And when you wake up, you say, "Was he there?"

Once he has come into your dream, that's the first step, and it's the major one. You've got to get him to appear at least once. Then once he appears, even if it's only for a second, now you can paint a picture, and paste a picture on your ceiling of him. Have pictures all around with lit candles, and light incense to him five times a day, and say "Come to me in my dreams, come to me in my dreams," etc. Do all sorts of rituals, all sorts of things in your life to remind you that this is the soul who's going to give you the information you desire and need and are worthy of.

Once he comes in, you change the mantra, and the new mantra becomes, *"Speak to me."* Which is to say, he's already in your dream now, he's already entered your subconscious mind, so now you can say, *"Speak to me, speak to me, speak to me...say something."* All right? Then once he speaks to you, even if just once, then you change the mantra to the third and final time, and the mantra becomes, in English, "Teach me such-and-such." It might be astrology, or karma, or whatever. But keep it as simple as you can.

RAY: Can it be a general thing, such as "teach me about life"?

KRIYANANDA: The more specific it is, the easier it is to crystallize. How would you say that to a college professor? You know you have to get it into a simple phrase which is clear and concise. If you can't, your mind has not gelled it and the entity will not speak to you specifically, he'll just ramble. So the more specific you can say, "Teach me," or "Show me," the better. And then you keep that. If he comes in your dream once, he can come again, he can speak again, and might ask him something else. That third stage is the most difficult. But if I were trying to get an entity to speak to me, this would be the technique I would actually use.

There are other techniques besides these, but this last one I've given you is probably the best and the safest, because there's nothing involved but verbal ritual, so there's no real way you can get into any difficulty. Okay?

RAY: I'm wondering if there any way to tell if the being who finally comes to you is a figment of your own imagination or is really "real," if you know what I mean.

KRIYANANDA: It doesn't matter.

RAY: But one is much more objective and "real," while the other one is more subjective. Even though they're both connected to your imagination, one of those has a reality outside of one's imagination, doesn't it?

KRIYANANDA: Respectfully, I know what you're saying, and I appreciate that, and it's a genuine problem, philosophically. But what *I'm* saying is, there *is* no "inner world," there is no "outer world," there really isn't. There's only o*ne world.*

RAY: I've been grappling lately with regrets over past mistakes I've made over the years, with feelings of guilt that are still lingering in my mind. For example it have to do with something I said to someone years ago that hurt someone's feelings, but I've lost touch with that person now, or they've died, so I can't go back and work it out with them. I feel almost like these things build up in my subconscious and weigh me down, like barnacles on a ship. My question is, what are some ways of resolving those feelings? Is it a matter of meditation, or prayer, or what?

KRIYANANDA: There are a number of things you can do, but here's a simple one. Find a space to sit and reflect, and think of the thought or feeling you're wanting to let go of, and then in your mind's eye visualize one of those old scythes—remember the two-handed scythes? And then you do this (sweeping motion, as if cutting something down)—it's as though you're cutting down any weeds that have grown from that five day-old or fifty-day old thought pattern.

RAY: Then what do you do with those emotional weeds once you've cut them off?

KRIYANANDA: You may think they'll grow back again, but once they're cut they really won't. Symbolically, they're cut forever. Alright? But another thing you can do is more of a meditative technique, and let's take your example of having said something that hurt another person's feelings. You close your eyes and visualize the person there in front of you, and you say to them whatever you feel you need say to them. You might say, "I didn't mean it that way," or "I sincerely apologize for having said that," or whatever it is you want to say. And you can do that whether the person is living or dead.

A third thing you can do to offset that emotion is to visualize the person and then ask yourself, *what color was the thought or the force?* Let's assume that it was a nasty "Martian" statement, as an example, a very harsh or angry statement. In that case what you threw at them was a red thought form, and so what you need to do is, with eyes closed, visualize the aura around the person, and their surrounding environment, being the opposite, complimentary color, probably blue. Because of my own color blindness, I would prefer just to think of something like a peaceful green or peaceful blue. In other words, just overriding the red. Or if the thought form was a very Saturnian black color, then you can visualize the person's aura being highly highly intensified in a colorful way.

The other thing I know you can do is less mystical but very effective, and that is prayer. Pray that that person forgives you, that God forgives you, and that you forgive you.

There are still other techniques, but hopefully these will help.

RAY: Shelly talks about the importance of being able to "think a new thought you haven't thought before." Why is that so important?

KRIYANANDA: Because we're so locked in by our memories and karmas, and that keeps us from moving forward. The idea is to get beyond that barrier, and that *is* a barrier.

If I can extend the point a little bit, this is what happens when the individual drives out into the astral world. They get locked in their own world—"Oh, God has got four heads!" Or, "God's a jealous god, and he's a monster!" He's locked inside all the memory tracks of his own subjective ego and fears and hatreds and selfishnesses and so forth.

And so the idea is to somehow get a thought that is *so* galactic that you couldn't possibly be in your own memory track. You see? Then all of the sudden you're in cosmic consciousness. It's one way to force yourself past the barrier of the memory track. So that's one of the approaches which the gjani yogi uses, with their path of knowledge, and it has tremendous implications. I'll say it another way: *you cannot hold a thought that is "not yours" and still remain you.*

RAY: But how do you know if a thought isn't yours?

KRIYANANDA: If you have a thought that isn't yours, it will throw you into a kind of samadhi, it'll essentially throw you out of your body. To say it a little differently, it'll throw you into an artistic creative state where you essentially lose awareness of this world. Now, you may be aware of the canvas, and the brush, or the music, but everything else, including your body, will have fallen away. Totally.

At one point during my studies I came into contact with an individual who I learned was dabbling in black magic—that is, practices ostensibly designed to manipulate or harm others. Though we were casual friends at the time, I became disturbed by what he was doing, and decided to keep my distance from him. According to a mutual acquaintance of ours, that upset him—and strangely enough, shortly afterwards I woke up feeling as though I was enveloped in a dark cloud. For several days I felt both physically and emotionally ill. I'd never experienced anything quite like this before, and strongly sensed this fellow might be directing negative energies towards me, especially since I knew he was dabbling in these sorts of practices.

Shortly afterwards, I told Kriyananda about the incident, and asked how someone can protect him or herself from possible "dark" influences like that. He said we're definitely affected by the thought-forms of others—especially if we allow ourselves to become relative to them, and mentioned the example of a judge sentencing criminals to sentences in the courtroom. "He may not consciously realize it, but the judge's unconscious is picking up those negative thoughts from the criminals he's sentencing. Imagine the impact that must have on him over time."

He then related a personal anecdote of his own, about a "psychic attack" he experienced himself once. Several years earlier he discovered that an individual who held a grudge against him had cast a curse on him—one that could prove extremely harmful if not counteracted. How did he deal with it, I asked? "I meditated on sending unselfish love towards him for three days." Was became of the situation, and the man, I wondered? "At the end of those three days he fell down the stairs and broke his neck," Kriyananda answered. It was obvious it was never Kriyananda's aim to harm the man, simply to rebuff his negative intentions; however those negative energies ricochet'd back on their point of origin.

RAY: What is the difference between meditation and astral projection, or astral awareness?

KRIYANANDA: The difference is that astral projection is not a balancing of consciousness, although by its very nature it does necessitate a *certain* degree of balancing. Basically, you are merely projecting your consciousness out to another realm, another part of yourself, in truth. But in deep meditation, you reach a point deep in your being where you are not only aware of your astral existence, but of your waking awareness and your balanced awareness as well.

RAY: I wonder if there's anything in the horoscope to indicate whether someone is an "old soul"? My guess is that it might be shown by a lot of Saturn aspects, either good or bad. But what do you think?

KRIYANANDA: That is definitely one way. Or, if there are a lot of aspects to the outer planets. For instance, you could split your ten planets in half, so to speak, between the inner five bodies (Sun, Moon, Mercury, Venus and Mars) and the outer five (Jupiter, Saturn, Uranus, Neptune and Pluto), and the older souls will tend to have far more aspects to the outer planets, regardless of whether those aspects are "good" or "bad." So that's one way. Not the shrewdest approach, perhaps, but fairly dependable in terms of determining old souls. If you have no aspects to those inner planets but the outer planets have tons of aspects, that would be a real indicator of an old-timer, someone who has been here and has been working off his or her karma.

RAY: But let's say the person has *no* real aspects to the outer planets, presuming that's even possible. What would that tend to indicate?

KRIYANANDA: That would tend to indicate it's a relatively new soul. "Tend to" is the operative phrase. Now, things are obviously a bit different with Hindu astrology, where you're only using the seven visible planets—you know the old phrase, "pass not the ring of Saturn." Also, an accumulation of planets in the first and second houses, or the first and second zodiacal signs, that's also supposed to be an indicator of a new soul coming in, or at least coming into *a new system*. My horoscope shows that, actually, in terms of the signs, anyway. Whereas my wife Joanna has a heavy accumulation of planets in the last two or three signs, Aquarius and Pisces, which is supposed to indicate a soul who's been in this segment a long, long time.

RAY: You run into strange overlaps sometimes, like a person who has lots of planets in Aries, for instance, but they're all trined out to Saturn, or opposing or squaring Saturn.

KRIYANANDA: It doesn't matter. The way we're talking here is, if a person has lots of planets in Aries, that is a new soul *in this segment of the universe*—and there's the key. Not a "new soul" in the ultimate sense, but a new soul *in this segment of the universe,* however you choose to define "this segment of the universe." It really wouldn't matter whether those planets are squared or trined. Square aspects would simply indicate they've brought a lot of difficult karma—using very simple terms—from another universe.

RAY: And if a person had a large number of planets in Pisces?

KRIYANANDA: That would tend to indicate an old soul who is about to leave, to depart from this segment of the universe. They've been here a *long* time. Now, you know, they could have ten squares, meaning they've really screwed up somewhere, using very simple language, or they've just not been able to really master their soul. And perhaps they have to get out of this solar system or this planet and come back in a different way and with a different direction. But they're at a crucial transition point.

RAY: What do you do say when you see someone who has difficult aspects coming up in their horoscope, and they tell you they want to start some important project, and they ask, "Should I do this, or shouldn't I?"

KRIYANANDA: You ask them, "Do you really *want* to do it? Is it valuable to you?" Because all the horoscope says is, it'll be a helluva battle. If you feel that what you want to do is really meaningful to you, or meaningful to mankind, then charge forward. But know it will be a tough, tough battle.

―――

One of our conversations took place on the heels of a personal tragedy Kriyananda had just experienced, and he seemed unusually open in his comments with me that time. At one point in that exchange I brought up the subject of his own teacher, Shelly, and how he benefitted from that relationship in the midst of such trials as this.

RAY: It's a blessing having a guru at times like this, isn't it?

KRIYANANDA: Yeah, he's been a damn blessing in my life, he really, really has. A *tough* son of a bitch, but I love him. He really is a Scorpio, and he frustrates the hell out of me sometimes, and he enjoys doing it (laughs loudly). But I guess that's what I need (smiles).

I really love him, and like he said to me once, when we were talking about gurus and his own guru, "You know, Yogananda was more of a father to me than my own father." And of course I lost *my* own father when I was three or four years old, and when I was six I had a stepfather who was a good man, he really was, but he was....unexpressive. The only thing he ever really said to me in all the years and decades I knew him was the time I'd just come back from the Korean War (where Kriyananda had been a battlefield medic) and he asked me, "Well, what do you think of shoot-em-up-bang-bang *now*, Melvin?" He was referring to playing with real guns in a real war, obviously. That told me he had been thinking an awful lot all those years. And that's the only statement he ever really made to me.

And you know, Shelly's been more of a father to me than both of *my* fathers. He's given me a great deal, and I'm really very, very fortunate.

RAY: I've been extremely tired lately, exhausted all the time, and I'm wondering what might be causing that?

KRIYANANDA: Has this been going on a long time?

RAY: Quite a while at this point.

KRIYANANDA: What is your Sun sign, if you don't mind my asking?

RAY: Gemini.

KRIYANANDA: And what's your Ascendant?

RAY: Virgo.

KRIYANANDA: Well, if this has been a long-term thing, then I'd say you probably made the same mistake I made: you came in with a Virgo Ascendant! (laughs) To be honest, that's a very constrictive symbol, a very 'earth plane'-type constriction. As an Ascending sign, Virgo can be a depleting energy symbol, and a difficult one to have on your Ascendant in that regard, especially if you don't have a lot of fire in your horoscope.

So I would say that you're *psychologically* depleted, in a larger sense, because you have a conflict in your soul. Whether you have two million questions that there are no real satisfactory answers to, like I used to have, or two million *exciting* questions, to which you will find the answers—and now you only have three million! And so you answer those and you wind up with five million. You understand?

You're playing in a Virgo game which, if you'll permit me, I played as well. Understand, I'm not criticizing! But it's exhausting, you're wearing the mind out, you're thinking too hard, whether you know it or not. You're exhausting your mind-body complex because of what I call *think, think, think*. Because there *is* no answer. You may get the answer to five million questions, but then you'll come up with *ten million* questions. And I'm not saying there hasn't been some great satisfaction in my life when I've had questions answered in my life, where I've said, "Wow!!!" It's great, exciting, I know. But then you all of a sudden think of ten more questions.

RAY: So the way around that is...?

KRIYANANDA: The way around that is to *think less*. Many Virgo types, by the way, are worriers. I don't know if you know that or not. And that can be very depleting also. They go together, really.

⇌

RAY: As you know, there's a viewpoint which says that if things are going well in your life, it's a sign that you must be living in spiritual harmony, and if things go wrong and your life falls into pieces, it's a sign that you're out of balance, and that you must not be spiritual.

KRIYANANDA: Yeah...that's where religion got born. Religion likes to say, "If I'm thinking all good things, all sorts of good things will come my way. But if my thoughts aren't good, then things will go bad." Now, I'm an old man, and one of the benefits from growing older is you get to see a lot of people over a lot of decades. In Kriya

Yoga, if I can go back to my foundation, this is what I have seen: a man or woman will be walking along, and all of the sudden in their chakras they'll have a Jupiter trine firing in their horoscope; they have a positive piece of karma fire in their life, in other words, a good astrological aspect. And that good Jupiter aspect will usually bring in some happiness, some bubbliness, but also some good food, some money, maybe some sex. And so they conclude, 'Oh, the one came after the other, therefore it was caused, I must have caused it!" In philosophy, that's called *hoc proper hoc.* Meaning it may have come after but it wasn't caused by it. Okay?

But all of a sudden, a more difficult piece of karma crops up, a difficult Saturn aspect comes into a person's life, and when that happens, it can take things away from us, and even make us crabby. So then we think, "Oh, I've had crabby thoughts"—and by the time we're aware of the crabby thoughts, we say, "It must be because I'm crabby that the good things have gone away..."

Now, the Tao master would say, "I'm old, and I've seen good or bad, but whether they're coming or leaving, *I'm always me."* Maybe that's a bit too concise, too curt. In other words, it is possible to have a bad Saturn, a difficult piece of karma firing, and yet still be bubbly and warm and patient and understanding, all from an inner awareness of yourself. Everything else may be going to hell, but you're still warm and patient and understanding.

You see, you're not responsible for bringing wealth or success into your life. In simple terms, you're responsible to be *happy,* to be *compassionate.* In which case you really *have* "won." No one says you should master the universe! People try to possess fame and wealth, and the answer to that is, if it comes in, fine. But know that it will leave tomorrow. And if it does, don't cry too hard, it will come again. Night, day, night, day, winter, summer, winter, summer.

Or I can put it like this. Mahatma Gandhi died, okay? My friend Sitting Bull died. My friend Jesus died. My friend Buddha died. And eventually I'm going to die. But what has that got to do with truth, with life, or the Tao? Everything, actually. That which is born sustains for a moment, then it dies. You have no control over the stars, you have no control over your loved ones, your family, your friends. I'm not even too sure we have any control over *us*. But what *ought* to be done is to put forth the effort to be in control. And to be in control necessitates the understanding that I can do nothing about those who die. I can do nothing about those who are violent. I know that those who are violent will bring hatred upon themselves. And more violent people shall rise up to crush *them*, and still more violent people shall rise to crush *them*, and so on, until you have nothing but a crushed universe. But what will remain is the soul that is incapable of being crushed.

But that soul incapable of being crushed won't rebuild the world; he or she will just continue to *live*. Now, someone may see how they live, and emulate that living, but it's not going to change the nature of the world. Religion says it will, of course. And religion will incite violence and a lot of other things, to make sure it does happen. But the history of the world is the history of religious wars. And that's as straight and honest as I can put it. You can check it yourself if I'm right or wrong, but fifty years down the line you'll be able to see it quite clearly—not so much from your life, but from your blessedness of being able to observe many people around you going through what we call "the cycle."

No matter how tightly I keep the "sun" lit in my head, the other sun out there goes down. No matter how tightly I keep the "full moon" in my head full, that other one up there keeps waxing and waning. I don't know what God's doing, all I really have to be concerned about is what *I* am doing. And again, that's a mystical statement, which can easily be misunderstood.

Shortly before finishing this book, I became aware of several transcripts of interviews with Kriyananda I hadn't seen before, conducted by Sharon

Steffensen. Besides containing helpful advice, they shed interesting light on Kriyananda's early life and studies, so I've chosen to include some excerpts from those interviews to close off this volume. I've edited these slightly for purposes of clarity.

QUESTION: What is the most important thing a person should know?

KRIYANANDA: That they can find answers for themselves, that they don't need teachers, gurus, priests, rabbis. As my guru said to me, "No one should have greater interest in me than me," No on would have greater interest in you than you. And so that you—whoever that you is—should pick up the search. So I think the answer is, we can find the answers. Life is knowable.

QUESTION: And how would you tell someone to find those answers?

KRIYANADA: I think the answer begins by, if they say they're really interested, you ask, "Are you sure you're really interested?" And if they say, "Yes, I'm really interested," you say, "Okay, show me, or show yourself that you're really interested by becoming self-disciplined, more self-disciplined." And then by becoming even more self-disciplined, which means getting further and further away from emotionality and getting rid of your emotional vested interests trying to prove yoga is the best or my guru is the greatest or anything of this nature, but simply looking for answers, recognizing that there are many, many, many, different paths along the way.

We have 90 years. We spend 30 years growing up, 30 years dying, so it gives us only 30 years. Of those, 10 are spent in sleep, and of the remaining 10 years those are at work. So we basically have 10 years to achieve any real accomplishments. So the third level is to therefore try to get one's economic base settled, so one is not tied down to a 9 to 5 for the rest of one's life. Something like 70% of the people who are retired in America are dependent upon financial help from family or government or otherwise. Only about 30% are not needing help, and most of those are just barely getting by. So the point of that third level, is to establish some sort of financial base where we can have more time and less effort to think, to reflect, to meditate, and to break free from the negative karma. And the fourth level is obviously to start breaking free from past-life karma.

QUESTION: So the goal of life, you feel would be to become more disciplined?

KRIYANANDA: I think that's a different question. To me, the goal of life is to become free, in simple language, to become free from our ignorance, our own forgetfulness, our own selfishness. On a second level, it is simply to stop hurting the world, people, the entities, life forms. Stop doing harm to them. And the next level is to start doing good for them, to help them. Not to interfere in their lives, not to meddle in their lives, but basically to do good. The goal is to become free, to become enlightened.

QUESTION: What was your childhood like?

KRIYANANDA: My father died when we were a few years old, my mother was left during the depression with three sons. Basically from that particular standpoint, she felt her son's should have a father, so she married a man to give us a father. She felts that was important, for sons to have a father. He turned out to be a wonderful step-father, a very good and highly evolved soul. But unfortunately, shortly after she married him, a week later, there were eight or ten children that came in from two previous marriages that he had had. And so the family grew to be 11 plus a mother and a father in one short week. During the depression time, between my two brothers and I, plus the eight or nine step-siblings, it was a pretty tough time growing up. I was sociologically in the middle and the attention goes to the older or younger children. The middle children seem to get lost. In my case, I found it to be a blessing because it gave me time to think and reflect and have a small universe of my own to examine.

As a young child I was very introverted. Introverted people think a great deal. They feel a great deal and are very sensitive to slight changes. And that led me to be more aware of people's emotions and how to understand them. I used to ask people, do you dream, do you dream in color, do your dream in dimensions? Do you see faces, do you see the things over in the corner, do you feel this vibration, do you smell this odor? And they never did. So I thought maybe there was something wrong with me.

Once I realized there were certain types of people, that I was not alone, there were other types of people like me, called mystics. Trying to understand that a great deal of pain in the world was not caused by God, but really caused by bad attitude, by being blind, by being greedy, by being heavily blinded attached to something—"my wife, my house, my car"—was really the source. So that drove me deeper and deeper into searching for peace and quiet, which I think I found at a fairly young age, and I realized at that particular point that I really was a teacher, I wanted to be a teacher to try to help remove their pain.

If I can jump forward, it was decades later that I recognized that people didn't want to get out of their pain. They enjoyed their pain. "Look how great I am, see how I am suffering." And it came back really to, "See how God has suffered. If I suffer, I am like God." Secondly, I realized a decade or two later that really people didn't want to put in any effort. They were waiting for God to save them. They were waiting for someone else to help them. They did not want to do it themselves.

QUESTION: So your major in college was chemistry?

KRIYANANDA: I started off in chemistry, mathematics and physics. And as I went along, I went back and took a little more, and I realized that wasn't where it's at. So I switched over to a philosophy major. And that was not very satisfying, it really honestly wasn't. So from there I realized that something's missing, and they had a couple of courses open up in terms of Eastern philosophy, Eastern religion. That really turned me on. That was what I had been looking for.

So I took everything there that they had to offer. I realized it made sense. I felt at home. After I went through that, I graduated. Because I had switched at the last minute, my degree was in philosophy, even though I has more subjects in physical sciences than philosophy.

QUESTION: So what did you do after college?

KRIYANANDA: After college, I decided to go to India and study. And I decided to work to be able to stay for awhile. Obviously, the easiest job to get in the business world was in chemistry and physics. There were more needs in those days for chemists, so they hired me as a chemist. I worked for a number of years and started accumulating money to go to India.

QUESTION: Where did you go in India?

KRIYANANDA: I traveled the length and breadth of India. I guess as far as the southern tip, Katchipurim all the way up to the Amritar, which is far north, and then Calcutta, all the way over to Bombay. So I made sort of a grand cross, as it used to be called, just traveling and trying to learn and study, that sort of thing. I didn't pick up any gurus or anything of this nature. I just tried to get information and was obviously looking for books, but there were not really books there. Most of those that I met were *sanyasis*, yogis on the road, Shaivites. They would talk to you and pass on communicative information.

QUESTION: When you came back, did you start giving lectures?

KRIYANANDA: Yes, people started asking questions of me. There had to be some reason why that happened. I opened up my house, I believe it was on Thursdays. I had a house on South Woodlawn. And we had people come in. There were about a dozen or so. I'd give a lecture for 45 minutes or an hour and we'd talk for about 45 minutes, just questions and answers. And then for whatever reason, we switched over to Sunday afternoon. Maybe the Sunday afternoon came first. We talked and talked and I lectured and answered questions. But then I found it was very hard to get them out of the house! They wanted to stay and stay. So then we switched to a Thursday night after work.

We were up on the third floor where one of the rooms had a library. There were about 12 people there, and we ran that for some time. We'd run from about 7 pm to 9:30 pm. We did that for a couple of years. It was between 12 and 20 people. And then they started telling me, "You should open a center." I don't know why I listened to them, but I opened a center in the Fine Arts Building on South Michigan Avenue, and within six months the 12 people who encouraged me to start it were no longer there. Obviously it didn't have the same flavor as being in a private home and talking intimately.

QUESTION: What were your days like with Shelly?

KRIYANANDA: Days were relatively simple. When he woke up he went through an hour ritual of breathing Kriya and we all had to be very quiet. During the rest of the day I basically chopped wood for the fireplace or tilled the garden. Very simple things like that.

The pattern was that after we ate, I helped with the dishes. Sometimes it was 7:30, sometimes 8:30 or 9:30. Around that time he had a signal. The way he held his hand and sort of looked at me and nodded, which meant I could ask a question. When that happened usually the other two children had gone to bed because they usually got up quite early. And Marjorie at that point went in the other room and closed the door and read a book.

And I'd ask a question and he'd think for five or ten seconds and then he would start answering the question. And he would continue to answer questions but if I nodded my head a little like I got sleepy, he'd say, "Well, it's time to go to bed." I'd say, "No, I'm wide awake." And he'd say, "Well, I'm sleepy." And that was the end of it. If I remained alert, he would talk until 7 the next morning without stopping. And then he would say to me, "and Kriyananda, that is the answer to your question which was…" and I'd stop for a minute and ask myself, "What the hell was the question I asked 7 hours ago." He had it indelibly in his head.

And this went on day after day. And so I realized I had to be very careful because if I asked a frivolous question, he'd spend eight hours on it. It became obvious there was one question per night. I had to take part of the time to study and think of which question was most vital.

QUESTION: What kind of questions did you ask him?

KRIYANANDA: Basically every question I could think of, to begin with, were based around questions like, "Why is everybody suffering? Why is everybody so stupid? Why is God mad at man?" Things of this nature. And the answers were profound.

But the answer was that God made us with our free will and he can't interfere with that free will. And he sits there sadly as we make a mess of our life. But that's how we grow, like a kid trying to learn how to walk. The parent sees the kid fall and skin his knees and doesn't want him to skin his knees. And it carries the kid and the kid will never learn how to walk.

QUESTION: Don't you think that now, people support yoga, they do want to hear that type of thing, they want to know truth now—but maybe not back then?

KRIYANADA: Well different organizations have different concepts and attract different types of people. Some want to know truth. I remember one day at the ashram, it was late in the evening and someone had come from New York. And he came to see Shelly. He said, "I have one question, Shelly. I've heard a lot about you."

And Shelly said, "Yes, what is the question?"

And I thought to myself, "Well, here goes an eight-hour discourse..."

And the man asked, "Is there a God?"

And without any hesitation, Shelly said, "Yes."

And the man stood up and said, "Thank you"—and then left. He just wanted a yes or no answer, he didn't want any explanation. And Shelly said a lot of people are like that, that they just want someone to reaffirm there is goodness and God. After that, they're no longer interested in the philosophy.

But he said to me, "You see, Kriyananda, not everyone is like you and I."

ABOUT THE AUTHOR

RAY GRASSE is a writer, astrologer, and photographer living in the Chicagoland area. He has authored four previous books, including *The Waking Dream, Signs of the Times, An Infinity of Gods,* and *Under a Sacred Sky*. He worked for ten years on the editorial staffs of Quest Books and *The Quest* magazine, and is currently associate editor of *The Mountain Astrologer* magazine. He graduated from the Art Institute of Chicago with a double major in filmmaking and painting, and studied with teachers in the Kriya Yoga and Zen traditions. For more information see www.raygrasse.com.